Epochs of Church History.

Edited by the Rev. M. CREIGHTON, M.A.,
Professor of Ecclesiastical History in the University of Cambridge.

Fcp. 8vo, price 80 cents each.

THE REFORMATION IN ENGLAND. By the Rev. Canon PERRY.
[*Now ready.*

THE ENGLISH CHURCH IN OTHER LANDS; or, THE SPIRITUAL EXPANSION OF ENGLAND. By Rev. H. W. TUCKER, M.A., Secretary to the Society for the Propagation of the Gospel.
[*Ready.*

The following is a List of the Volumes at present proposed:

THE GERMAN REFORMATION. By Rev. M. CREIGHTON, M.A., D.C.L., Professor of Ecclesiostial History in the University of Cambridge.

ENGLAND AND THE PAPACY. By Rev. W. HUNT, M.A., Trinity College, Oxford.

WYCLIF AND THE BEGINNINGS OF THE REFORMATION. By REGINALD LANE POOLE, M.A., Balliol College, Oxford.

THE CHURCH OF THE EARLY FATHERS. By Rev. A. PLUMMER, D.D., Master of University College, Durham.

THE ARIAN CONTROVERSY. By H. M. GWATKIN, M.A., Lecturer and late Fellow of St. John's College, Cambridge.

THE CHURCH AND THE ROMAN EMPIRE. By Rev. A. CARR, M.A., late Fellow of Oriel College, Oxford.

THE CHURCH AND THE EASTERN EMPIRE. By Rev. H. F. TOZER, M.A., Lecturer and late Fellow of Exeter College, Oxford.

THE RELIGIOUS REVIVAL IN THE EIGHTEENTH CENTURY. By Rev. J. H. OVERTON, M.A.

THE UNIVERSITY OF CAMBRIDGE. By J. BASS MULLINGER, M.A., Lecturer of St. John's College, Cambridge.

THE UNIVERSITY OF OXFORD.

CHURCH AND STATE IN MODERN TIMES.

THE REFORMATION IN ENGLAND.

THE WARS OF RELIGION.

THE COUNTER-REFORMATION.

ECCLESIASTICAL PROBLEMS IN ENGLAND, 1570-1660.

THE CHURCH AND THE TEUTONS.

CHRISTIANITY AND ISLAM.

HILDEBRAND AND HIS TIMES.

THE POPES AND THE HOHENSTAUFEN.

MONKS AND FRIARS.

London: LONGMANS, GREEN & CO.

NEW YORK:
ANSON D. F. RANDOLPH & COMPANY,
38 WEST TWENTY-THIRD STREET.

Epochs of Church History

EDITED BY THE

REV. MANDELL CREIGHTON, M.A.

THE

REFORMATION IN ENGLAND

HISTORY

OF THE

REFORMATION IN ENGLAND

BY

GEORGE G. PERRY, M.A.

CANON OF LINCOLN AND RECTOR OF WADDINGTON

24820

NEW YORK
ANSON D. F. RANDOLPH & COMPANY
38 WEST TWENTY-THIRD STREET

PREFACE.

In this little volume an attempt is made to give a clear and connected account of the religious and ecclesiastical changes through which the Church of England passed in the sixteenth century. In order to preserve this special character of the book, many aspects of the Reformation, and of the history of the Church during this period, are scarcely touched upon. My endeavour has been to keep steadily in view the progress of the National Church from its state of bondage to Rome, and its encumbrance with many superstitious doctrines and practices, to the commencement of a higher life, the acquisition of Catholic and scriptural formularies, and the enjoyment of greater freedom. Only such historical facts as are directly connected with this religious progress are here given. Ecclesiastical history may be written in many different ways, and it is not every period which is susceptible of such a treatment as this. But the Reformation was a great religious crisis in the life of the Church, and seems to demand a special treatment. The formation and growth of the Formularies with which English Churchmen are familiar, must ever be a subject of peculiar interest. It is hoped also that the simple narrative of the religious struggles and changes through which the Church of England passed during a period of more than forty years, may serve to remove the delusion, still too widely spread, that the Church of England is a body which was called into existence by some Act of Parliament in the sixteenth century. We may here see the National Church—not without many weaknesses, drawbacks, and errors—slowly and painfully shaking herself free from the obstructions which had long vexed her, and at length reaching a region of purer light.

As no references are given in the body of the work it may be desirable to state the principal sources from which it is compiled. These are:—Strype's 'Annals of the Reformation' and 'Lives of Archbishops Cranmer and Parker'; Collier's 'Ecclesiastical History'; Burnet's 'History of the Reformation'; Heylin's 'Ecclesia Restaurata'; Wilkins's 'Concilia Magnæ Britanniæ'; Cardwell's 'Synodalia'; 'Documentary

Annals' and 'Two Liturgies of Edward VI.'; Ellis's
'Original Letters'; Amos' 'Statutes of Reformation
Parliament'; Churton's 'Papers in British Magazine';
'The Phœnix' (containing an account of the English
Reformers abroad); Archæologia, vol. xviii.; the
'Original Letters' and 'Zürich Letters' (published by
the Parker Society); the 'Parker Correspondence';
'Suppression of the Monasteries' (Camden Society);
'Formularies of Faith in the Reign of Henry VIII.';
Camden's 'Life and Reign of Elizabeth'; the 'Elizabethan Formularies' (Parker Society); Hardwick on
the Articles; Foxe's 'Martyrology;' and numerous other
works.

CONTENTS.

CHAPTER I.

INTRODUCTORY.

PAGE

Causes of the Reformation—1. Religious; 2. Political; 3. Social—Character of the Reformation—National rights of the Church of England 1

CHAPTER II.

THE REFORMATION PARLIAMENT AND CONVOCATION, 1529–35.

Fall of Cardinal Wolsey—Wolsey inaugurator of radical reform—Three anti-clerical bills—Opposition of Bishop Fisher—The first blow against the supremacy of the Pope—Complaints of the Convocation—Petition of members of Parliament to the Pope—Proclamation against bulls from Rome—Royal supremacy voted by the clergy—The grievances of the Commons against the ordinaries—Answers of Convocation—The 'Submission of the clergy'—Convocation petitions against papal annates—Statute for restraint of appeals—Subsequent modification of the statute—The 'Consecration' statute—Visitatorial rights given to the Crown—Supremacy Act—First-fruits and tenths given to the Crown—Vote of the clergy against jurisdiction of the Pope 9

CHAPTER III.

THE ADVOCATES OF THE REFORMATION.

General desire for change in the religious status—Cambridge reformers—Hugh Latimer—His letter to the king—Made bishop of Worcester—Dr. Barnes—John Fryth—William Tyndale—His translation of the New Testament—Archbishop Cranmer—Thomas Crumwell—Affair of the Nun of Kent—The oath in the Succession Act—Condemnation of More and Fisher—The Court divines—The first English Bible—First reforming primer—Crumwell appointed vicar-general . . 18

CHAPTER IV.

FALL OF THE MONASTERIES, 1536-9.

Growth and character of the monastic system—Decay of the monasteries—Their suppression resolved upon—The passing of the Act—Commissioners to arrange for the demolition—The Pilgrimage of Grace—Disastrous effect of it on the greater monasteries—Cruelties of the dissolution—Amount of spoil obtained—Its appropriation—Transfer of the abbey lands to laymen—Evils resulting from this—Act to give the king chantries and collegiate property—Hard case of the ejected monks and nuns—Cruelties of the period 30

CHAPTER V.

RELIGIOUS PROGRESS DURING THE REIGN OF HENRY VIII., 1536-47.

The ancient Church services—Ignorance of the people—Bishop Latimer's sermon to the Convocation—The Ten Articles—Protest against proposed Council of Mantua—Diminution of holydays—First royal injunctions—Measures taken to influence the people—The making of the book, 'The Institution of a Christian Man'—Second English Bible—The

CONTENTS   xi

PAGE

'Great Bible'—The injunctions of 1538—Rifling of the tomb of St. Thomas—The king excommunicated—Attempt to procure a union between the Lutherans and the Church of England—Effects of this attempt on the king—The Six Article law—Obsequiousness of Cranmer and the clergy—Bloodthirsty proceedings of the latter part of the reign—Policy of the anti-reforming party—Formation of the 'Erudition of any Christian Man'—The king's primer—The liturgical revision—Bishop Gardiner—Thomas Crumwell—Character of the religious history of the period . . . 39

CHAPTER VI.

THE UNSETTLING CAUSED BY THE ACCESSION OF EDWARD VI., 1547-9.

Erastian policy of King Edward's council—The check of Convocation—First royal visitation—The homilies—The first Injunctions of Edward VI.—Gardiner and Bonner committed to prison—First English communion office—The proclamation for the new communion office—Violent legislation—Proclamations of the year 1548—Unauthorised services—Wild opinions 60

CHAPTER VII.

THE FIRST ENGLISH PRAYER-BOOK, 1549-50.

Cranmer's invitations to foreign reformers—Amount of influence of foreign reformers on English Prayer-book—The book mainly an adaptation of the ancient offices—Great value of the book—Approved by Convocation—Established by law—The preface—Unpleasing to the more violent reformers—To the common people—Attempts to give the book the character of the old services—Second royal visitation—Bishop Bonner deprived—The first reformed ordinal—Order to destroy the old service-books—Altars ordered to be removed 69

CHAPTER VIII.

THE DOCTRINAL CONFESSION AND MANUALS OF THIS REIGN, 1547–53.

Cranmer's homilies—The Lutheran catechism—Cranmer's treatise on the Eucharist—Formation of the Forty-two Articles—Poynet's catechism—The primer of 1553—Writings of reformers 80

CHAPTER IX.

THE SECOND ENGLISH PRAYER-BOOK, 1552–3.

Reformatio legum ecclesiasticarum—Cranmer and Ridley satisfied with first Prayer-book—John Hooper—Review of the first Prayer book—The second communion office—The Black Rubrick—Second Act of Uniformity 86

CHAPTER X.

THE LEGISLATION UNDER EDWARD VI., 1547–53.

Legislation of the first Parliament—Act to give the king free chapels and chantries—Marriage of clergy legalised—Act for securing tithes—Act for the removal of all images and pictures—Legislation of 1552—The Holydays Act—Confusion between sacred and secular things 95

CHAPTER XI.

CHURCH SPOLIATIONS AND MORALS, 1547–53.

Church spoliation not peculiar to the Reformation era—Various forms of church spoliation—The building of Somerset House—The commissioners under the Act for granting colleges, &c., to the king—Seizure of episcopal manors—Spoliation of benefices—Spoliation of churches—King Edward's benefactions—Burning of Joan Boucher—The morality of the period . 101

CHAPTER XII.

THE FIRST MEASURES OF RETALIATION, 1553-4.

Change by the accession of Mary—Character of the Queen—Release of the imprisoned bishops—Indifference of the people—Resistance of the Parliament—The Convocation of Canterbury—Exercise of the royal supremacy—Gardiner's policy—Measures against the reforming bishops . . . 113

CHAPTER XIII.

THE SPANISH REVENGE, 1554-8.

The Spanish divines—Bartholomeo de Carranza—Pedro de Soto—Villagarcia—Alphonso de Castro—Arrival of the papal legate and absolution of the nation—The Queen's determination to burn—The first commissioners—Hooper and Rogers—Rowland Taylor—John Bradford and Laurence Saunders—Bishop Farrar—Sermon of Alphonso de Castro—The bishops checked for slackness—Ridley and Latimer—Archbishop Cranmer—His recantations—Retracts his recantations—His execution—His character—Archdeacon Philpot—The bishops driven on unwillingly—Lay officers shrink from acting—Amount of the sufferers—Reformation advanced by the persecution—The Queen's benefactions—Misery of the period 120

CHAPTER XIV.

THE ENGLISH REFORMERS ABROAD, 1553-8.

Reformed congregations in England—The reformers who escaped—The English service at Frankfort—Others invited to Frankfort—Stipulation for use of the English Prayer-book—John Knox—Dispute as to the English Prayer-book—Calvin's opinion of the Prayer-book—Dr. Cox—Knox banished—New dissension on discipline—The Frankfort congregation becomes Presbyterian—The other English settlements—Action of the Geneva body—Spirit of the reformers who returned . 142

CHAPTER XV.

THE RECOVERY OF THE CHURCH OF ENGLAND, 1558-9.

Queen Elizabeth's religious policy—Proclamation about preaching—The recommendations given to Cecil—Elizabeth's own religious views—The question of the bringing back the reformed settlement—The commission to review the Prayer-book—Sir W. Cecil's questions—The proviso in the Act of Uniformity—The meeting of Parliament—Supremacy Act——The Act of Uniformity—The Elizabethan Prayer-book—The Latin Prayer-book 151

CHAPTER XVI.

THE BISHOPS AND CLERGY.

The difficulty of finding clergy for the reformed church—The Romish bishops and clergy—The Westminster disputation—The bishops before the Queen—Their treatment—The clergy who refused the Prayer-book—The new bishops—Archbishop Parker—His consecration—Consecration of other bishops—Poverty of the sees—Ordinations of clergy—Ordination of readers—Arrangements for lay readers—Scrupulousness of the new bishops 165

CHAPTER XVII.

THE DISCIPLINE, 1559–71.

Queen Elizabeth's injunctions—Clerical matrimony—Images in churches—Explanation of the royal supremacy—Prayer for the dead—Visitation of the commissioners—Bernard Gilpin—The 'Declaration'—The bishops' 'Interpretations'—Articles and declaration—The bishops not favourable to discipline—Debate on ceremonies in the Convocation—The Queen's letter to the primate—Archbishop Parker's 'Advertisements'—Opposition of some of the clergy—Reply of the London ministers—Growth and ill-effects of the controversy—The difficulties through which the church advanced . . . 176

CHAPTER XVIII.

THE DOCTRINAL CONFESSION, 1563–71.

The doctrinal confession not restored at first—Review of the Forty-two Articles—The articles before Convocation—The Queen's ratification—The clause in the twentieth article—Attempt to enforce subscription by law—The Act of 1571—The articles finally reviewed by the Convocation—Character of the subscription—The new homilies—Completion of the Reformation settlement 192

CHAPTER XIX.

THE DEFENCE OF THE REFORMATION.

Protests against Rome in earlier days—At length successful—The cause of obloquy against the Church of England—Defenders of the English church—Bishop Jewel—Richard Hooker—Dean Field—Archbishop Bramhall—The Protestant defence—William Chillingworth—Varieties of doctrine no just reproach to the Reformation—The reformed church unfairly censured for irregularities—Difficulty arising from the character of Elizabeth—The Reformation not chargeable with the cruelties exercised towards Roman Catholics—Its effects favourable to art and literature—Its effects on the Roman church 199

INDEX 215

HISTORY

OF THE

REFORMATION IN ENGLAND.

CHAPTER I.

INTRODUCTORY.

IN the great ecclesiastical revolution of the sixteenth century the Church of England reached at length that deliverance from the fetters of Rome for which she had been labouring and struggling, at various times, through many centuries. Having established and cleared her national rights, she was then able to enter upon a course of reformation and improvement in accordance with the teaching of the Scriptures and the primitive Church. But this was not done at once, nor without convulsions, reactions, errors, and harsh dealing.

It would indeed be impossible to find in all history a genuine record of any great revolution, either in Church or State, wherein all the agents had proceeded upon pure, disinterested motives—which was entirely uncontaminated by ambition, self-seeking, covetousness, or any of the lower motives of human actions. Certainly an exception to this cannot be claimed in favour of the English Reformation of the sixteenth century, whether we look at the usurping and tyrannical King, the timid and too subservient clergy, or the grasping and unprincipled laity. Yet reflection shows that there were advantages even in these evil features. Nothing less than the bold, overbearing temper of the King would have been adequate to head the movement which brought about the emancipation of England from the tyranny of Rome. A bolder struggle for ancient rights on the part of the clergy might have led to the utter apostasy of the State; and the covetous greed with which the laymen fell upon ecclesiastical property gave a stability to the work of change which it could not probably have acquired in any other way.

In estimating the immediate causes which brought about the great change which passed over the Church of England at this period, we may perceive that they were of various character. Some of the causes were religious, some political, some social. Of the first sort was the strong and faithful attachment to the writings and teaching of John Wycliffe and the Lollards, cherished by many persons, chiefly in humble positions, in spite of the persecutions to which they had been subjected. The Lollard opinions had survived and been handed down, though, as Lord Herbert observes, 'in so obscure and perplexed a manner that they served rather to show errors than to rectify them.' Their preservation had the effect, however, of making many dissatisfied with the teaching then prevalent in the Church, and ready to welcome a

Causes of the Reformation.
1. Religious causes

doctrinal change. The holders of these opinions were more or less persecuted by the bishops in the earlier days of Henry VIII., and persecution had its usual effect of increasing zeal for the persecuted opinions Then, in aid of this somewhat ignorant disaffection to the prevailing teaching, came the gradual leakage into England of the opinions of Luther. Luther's 'Babylonish Captivity' was published in 1520, and in March 1521 we find Archbishop Warham writing to Wolsey to tell him that Oxford was greatly infected with the heresies of Luther, and that he feared Cambridge was in no better plight. The Cardinal determined to make a holocaust of the heretical books, and it appears that a very large number of them were brought together and burned at St. Paul's (Aug. 1, 1521). The King's book against Luther quickly followed (Aug. 25), and the interest excited by this unusual proceeding, the daring reply of Luther, and the gross invective of Sir Thomas More, all tended to bring this controversy into marked prominence. There are indications that Cardinal Wolsey, though compelled officially to act against them, was yet somewhat of a favourer of the Lutheran views. He could not be induced cordially to approve of the King's book, and the divines whom he brought from Cambridge to be members of his new college at Oxford were, most of them, holders of Lutheran opinions. A vast stimulus was given to the reforming sentiment by the publication in 1526 at Worms, on the Rhine, of William Tyndale's translation into English of the New Testament. The bishops were immediately on the watch to prevent these books from being brought into England; but very large numbers eluded their vigilance, and in 1527 it was thought necessary to have a public burning in Cheapside of all the copies which could be found. At the same time a large number of reforming tracts and books were written by English refugees sheltered abroad, and imported into England. Of these the 'Supplication of Beggars,' written by Simon Fish, and brought into England in 1528, fell in exactly with the sentiment, now becoming very prevalent, as to the gross abuses upheld by ecclesiastics in connection with the doctrine of Purgatory. In this witty but scurrilous composition the whole of the fables about Purgatory, the efficacy of masses, and the value of indulgences are held up to ridicule; and so popular was it that Sir Thomas More thought it necessary at once to answer it by his 'Supplication of Souls.' The effect of this and the other books of a strongly reforming character dispersed through the country was that, before the commencement of the Reformation Parliament of November 1529, which is the true beginning of the English Reformation, public opinion was thoroughly leavened, and prepared for considerable changes in the religious status.

Probably, however, the religious forces at work would not have been sufficient to produce important results, nor strong enough to stand the test of a repressive persecution, had they not been supplemented by others of a political and social character. Among the chief of the political causes was, of course, the divorce case of the King and the introduction into power and influence, through Anne Boleyn, of a party whose interests were staked on taking up and maintaining a position hostile to the Pope and the

2. Political causes

Emperor. Henry VIII. had always been eager to assert his supremacy over ecclesiastical persons, as he had shown in 1516 in the case of Dr. Standish. Later in his reign he had been in treaty with the King of France to bring about the liberation of both Churches from Romish control. When, therefore, he was harassed above measure by the duplicity and tergiversation of Rome in the divorce case, he was well disposed to throw the weight of his authority on the side of the Reformation, though in his religious views he in no way varied from the prevalent Church teaching. A man of great abilities, and of a strongly autocratic temper, Henry was fully cognisant of the rights which had frequently been exercised by the Kings of England, and was perfectly determined to exert them. The proceedings of the Legatine Court at Blackfriars, which took place during the summer of 1529, and proved clearly to him that the Pope was playing with him, did not tend to make his temper more conciliatory towards the Church when Parliament met.

There were also social causes strongly at work in England at this period which were leading towards a change in the ecclesiastical position. It is evident that there was a most bitter feeling prevalent between clergy and laity. The vexations of the Church courts; their processes, where scarce even the semblance of justice was preserved; the heavy fines inflicted by them, and the inordinate use of the weapon of excommunication; the immunities of the clergy, defended by numberless Acts of Parliament; the absorption of almost all valuable State offices by Churchmen; the luxurious pomp of Wolsey and others, while the

3. Social causes

country was covered with gibbets bearing the bodies of poor wretches executed simply for the crime of begging—all these things tended to produce a hatred of Churchmen in the minds of the laity. Many of those who had not imbibed any of the reforming religious opinions had ceased to care about the old attractions of the Church. Pilgrimages, relics, winking Madonnas, and bleeding saints were a subject of ridicule. Erasmus, in his 'Colloquies' and 'Encomium Moriæ,' represents to us the sentiment of this class, who soon came to be known by the name of the *Ribauds*. The manifold grievances which the laity had, or thought they had, against the Church and Churchmen found expression in the Parliament of 1529.

And, besides these more vulgar complainants, there was a knot of superior men, not desiring a change of religion, nor even caring much about an improvement in Papal relations, but profoundly impressed with the gross ignorance which prevailed among the clergy, and earnestly desiring at almost any cost a reformation in learning. Of this coterie Cardinal Wolsey was the patron, and probably a sincere one. Erasmus was a valuable ally, rather from his love of learning than from any zeal for truth. Sir Thomas More and Bishop Fisher were members, though soon frightened away by their dread of heresy; but the most valuable and most sincere of them all was Dean Colet, too soon lost to the Church. Archbishop Warham and Bishop Foxe of Winchester may also be fairly described as members of this band of educational reformers. It will thus be seen that in 1529, when our History commences, a number of causes were at

[margin: Intellectual reformers]

work to prepare the ground for some considerable change in the condition of the Church. A vast mass of superstitious practices and strange semi-pagan teaching, had, during the Middle Ages, gathered round the great doctrines of Christianity. The remarkable work of Thomas Gascoigne [1] exhibits to us the religion of that period in a frightfully corrupted state. Men in England might not be able as yet to reach the exact standard of theological truth, but there were many who had sufficient moral sense to be repelled by gross abuses and manifest impostures, and light was gradually streaming into the land from various quarters.

In the changes and convulsions of the period there were divers unjust and evil things done, and many characters damaged; but, upon the whole, progress was maintained towards the perception of the true position of the Church of England, a purer doctrinal standard, a pruning away of the superstitious accessories of worship, an open Bible, and greater liberty of thought. In reaching these things the continuity of the National Church was not interfered with, the succession of bishops was not broken, nor did the sacraments cease to be administered. The process was gradual—subject indeed to many checks and vicissitudes; yet it never took the form of a revolution, but always maintained a conservative character.

Character of the Reformation

It was, in fact, but the continuation and successful development of the ancient struggle and contention of

---

[1] Thomas Gascoigne, a leading divine of the fifteenth century, composed a 'Theological Dictionary,' great part of which, under the name of *Loci e Libro Veritatum*, has lately been published by the Clarendon Press, with an able preface by Mr. T. Rogers, M.P.

the Church of the land. The English Reformation began with the assertion of the true position of the National Church as regards Rome. In times of weakness and ignorance the Bishop of Rome, having the prestige of the imperial city, had contrived to persuade Europe that it was his mission to be the autocrat over all the Churches. To this the English Church before the Conquest had yielded but a partial assent. But the Norman dynasty brought England more distinctly into the European family, and her Churchmen adopted the prevailing tone of subjection to the inordinate claims of Rome. There were, however, frequent protests against this. The founder of the dynasty, William I., claimed for himself a complete ecclesiastical supremacy. He refused to do homage to the Pope for the realm of England, on the ground that his predecessors had never done so, and he would not allow Papal Bulls to run in his kingdom without his approval first obtained. A successor, Henry II., brought about at Clarendon the same assertion of the rights of the National Church as was afterwards embodied in the Statute of Appeals. This was repeated by King John, who told the Pope that 'his prelates in England were sufficiently furnished with a full provision of all learning, and he had no need to go a-begging to foreigners for justice and judgment.' During the reigns of Edward III. and Richard II. no less than six Acts of Parliament asserted the illegality of the interference of the Pope with the temporalties of the English Church; and when, in the next century, an overbearing Pope (Martin V.) demanded of the Crown the repeal of these obnoxious statutes, the Commons replied by presenting

National rights of the Church of England

a petition to the King praying him to uphold the liberties of the Church of England against Papal aggressions. The legislation, therefore, of the Reformation Parliament was not of altogether a novel character, but only the revival of that which, for somewhat more than a century, during the troubles and weakness of the Wars of the Roses, had been in abeyance.

CHAPTER II.

THE REFORMATION PARLIAMENT AND CONVOCATION.

1529-1535.

WHEN the Parliament met on November 3, 1529, all men's minds were full of the fall of Cardinal Wolsey.

Fall of Cardinal Wolsey Shortly before this the King had caused the Great Seal to be taken from him by the Dukes of Norfolk and Suffolk, had seized his costly goods and furniture, and sent him in disgrace to Esher. The Cardinal's influence had been so great that this was almost equivalent to a revolution. There was a baseness in men's characters at this time, and a mean subservience to the King's will, which were now remarkably displayed. The Cardinal had been a great minister, with many excellent qualities; but he, too, had shown a sycophantic deference to Henry's whims, and had behaved very badly to Queen Catherine in the divorce case. Now the same evil spirit was displayed towards himself. Sir Thomas More thought it consistent with his high office as Chancellor to inveigh against the fallen man as a 'rotten sheep,' and a Bill of frivolous indictment was brought into the House of Lords against him. Wolsey passes from the scene eating his great heart in misery, at the loss of royal favour, and dying wretchedly at Leicester Abbey (November 30, 1530).

But it should not be forgotten that Wolsey, the great Churchman, was the inaugurator of that bold policy of dealing with the old religious foundations, with a view to employing their revenues for more useful purposes. which afterwards ran into so much riot and excess. He procured from the Pope two Bulls for suppressing monasteries, in order to endow his Colleges of Oxford and Ipswich, and two other Bulls (1528, 1529) for suppressing monasteries for the foundation of bishoprics. The latter Bull seems to give the Cardinal a general power of using any or all abbeys for the erection of sees, and it is apparently on this ground that a paper was drawn up by the King specifying twenty-one new sees which it would be desirable to found out of monasteries. Wolsey was therefore the beginner of the vigorous attack on the old ecclesiastical system which was now commenced.

Wolsey, inaugurator of radical Reform

Immediately on the opening of Parliament three Bills directed against the clergy were brought in and passed by the Commons. The first of these regulated the fees payable in the Church courts for the probate of wills. The second fixed the amount which might be claimed for mortuary fees. The third was directed against pluralities, non-residence, and clerical farming. These Bills, when brought into the Lords, excited great indignation among the bishops. The most prominent among these was Fisher, Bishop of

Three anti-clerical Bills

Rochester, a man of saintly life but somewhat narrow mind. He had been confessor to Queen Catherine and was strongly opposed to the divorce. He now attacked the proceedings of the Commons with vehemence and accused them of wanting to imitate the heretics of Bohemia. What followed clearly indicated the feeling of the laymen towards the ecclesiastics. The Commons, headed by their Speaker, complained to the King. The Bishop was sent for by Henry, and the Archbishop and six other bishops were bidden to accompany him. He was called on for a public apology, and made one, which certainly looks very feeble, and which the Commons freely stigmatised as a 'blind excuse.' As in the House of Lords the spiritual peers were in a majority, the Bills sent up from the Commons were not able to pass until they had been considerably modified; and the Bill against pluralities, which made it penal to obtain a license from Rome, was absolutely condemned. But at that period the King had great power in controlling the action of Parliament, and he was bent on obtaining the passing of this Bill, the importance of which he clearly saw. He called a meeting of eight members of each House. There was 'sore debating' (as the chronicler Hall tells us), but the bishops were at last obliged to yield and the Bill passed.

Opposition of Bishop Fisher

It was the first blow struck against the Pope's supremacy at this time, and was conceived exactly in the spirit of the Provisors and Præmunire Statutes of the fourteenth century. It enacted heavy fines against any clerk who should obtain from Rome a license for holding benefices in

The first blow against the supremacy of the Pope

plurality, or for non-residence, and the sequestration of the benefices obtained under such license. Naturally so rude an interference of the lay power provoked the clergy of the Convocation of Canterbury. They complain that, in spite of the liberties conceded to them by ancient charters, they are much oppressed by the uncertain action of the Statute of Præmunire, and that the law just passed, without their being consulted, was a grievous act of tyranny, the authors of which deserved excommunication. The first session of this Parliament terminated, leaving things in a very embittered state between the clergy and laity. During the year 1530 there was no regular session of Parliament, but a petition was addressed to the Pope as from the Parliament, signed by two archbishops, two dukes, two marquesses, thirteen earls, four bishops, twenty-six barons, twenty-two abbots, and eleven knights and doctors of Parliament, praying for a speedy settlement of the divorce suit. The Pope answered this petition somewhat angrily, blaming the signers for their interference. The King replied by a proclamation making it penal to introduce Bulls from Rome.

Complaints of the Convocation

Petition of members of Parliament to the Pope

The Parliament met on January 16, 1531. The opinions of the Universities in favour of the divorce were read. An Act of excessive severity against proctors and pardoners, who sold indulgences from Rome, was passed. The whole of the clergy of England had been found guilty under the Statute of Præmunire for having submitted to the legislative authority of Wolsey. They were informed by the judges, in a communication to the Convocation

Proclamation against Bulls from Rome

of Canterbury, that they would be pardoned on voting a subsidy, if the subsidy was accompanied by a formal admission of the King's supremacy. After many negotiations and much unwillingness on the part of the Canterbury Convocation, that body voted (February 11, 1531) to address the King as 'the singular protector, the only and supreme lord, and, as far as is permitted by the law of Christ, even the supreme head of the Church of England.' Upon this, and after voting a subsidy of 100,044*l.* 8*s.* 8*d.*, the clergy of the southern province were 'pardoned.' The northern province stood out longer against the acknowledgment of the supremacy, but finally (May 4) admitted it, and voted a subsidy of 18,040*l.* 0*s.* 10*d.* Upon this they also were pardoned. This 'acknowledgment of the royal supremacy' was afterwards embodied in an Act of Parliament, but not in the exact terms in which it was made, the phrase 'as far as is permitted by the law of Christ' being omitted.

Royal supremacy voted by the clergy

In the session of Parliament of January 1532 several Bills abridging the power and privileges of the clergy were brought in, and on March 18 the Commons laid before the King their paper of 'grievances' against the ordinaries. These were: (1) That canons were made in Convocation without the royal assent, and enforced to the derogation of the royal authority. (2) That the Archbishop only allowed certain proctors to plead in his court. (3) That the laity were vexed in proceedings for discipline. (4) That the fees of ecclesiastical courts were excessive. (5) That the clergy exacted fees for sacraments

The grievances of the Commons against the ordinaries

and sacramentals. (6) That testamentary proceedings were very troublesome and expensive. (7) That the ordinaries required inordinate fees for induction and institution. (8) That patronage was misused. (9) That the number of holy days was excessive. (10) That men were sent to prison without knowing the charge against them. (11) That they had no chance of recovering damages for false charges. (12) That men were examined subtilly and entrapped into heretical statements. They prayed the King to provide such remedies as might reconcile and bring into unity his subjects, secular and spiritual.

The Convocation replied, the Bishop of Winchester (Gardiner) being appointed to revise the answer. The King gave it to the Speaker of the House of Commons with a contemptuous description of it. The Convocation, finding that it was not acceptable, drew up another answer, which specially addressed itself to the point of the right of the clergy to make canons, independently of the royal assent. They claimed this right to belong to them in all matters connected with faith, doctrine, and discipline.

Answers of Convocation

This had the effect of rousing the King's autocratic spirit. He sent down to the Convocation by Bishop Edward Fox, his almoner, three articles, to which he required the clergy to subscribe. The first of these was: (1) That no constitution or canon should hereafter be enacted and put forth by the clergy without the King's consent. (2) That the ancient canons should be revised and amended by a Commission to be appointed by the King. (3) That the ancient canons not objected to by the Commission

The 'submission of the clergy'

should stand good when ratified by the King's approval. This was to put the whole of the ecclesiastical laws into a position of absolute dependence upon the King's will, and was naturally very distasteful to the clergy. The Lower House of the Canterbury Convocation, however, accepted it. But the Upper House, by inserting the word *new* into the first clause (May 16), still left the old constitutions untouched until condemned by the Commission. The work of this Commission, afterwards reappointed, was never legally sanctioned and has no binding force. Consequently neither the 'submission of the clergy' in their Convocation, nor the Act of Parliament which embodied it, has had the effect of abrogating the ancient canons of the Church of England, which, when not contrariant to statute law, are in force still. The important points established by the 'submission of the clergy' and the Act of Parliament which embodied it were: (1) That Convocation must always henceforth originate with the King's writ to the Archbishop. (2) That no new canon passed by it can be promulged without the royal sanction. These were cardinal points in formulating and settling the royal supremacy.

If the clergy accepted these things grudgingly, it does not appear that they were actuated in doing so by any special regard for the Pope and his interests; for the Convocation petitioned the King to demand from the Pope the surrender of his claim to annates (the first year's income of benefices) and other pecuniary claims, and if he should refuse, 'that then the obedience of the King and his people be withdrawn from the See of Rome.' This petition

Convocation petition against Papal annates

was either suggested by, or was the foundation of, the Act of Parliament abolishing annates and Papal fees. This Act was remarkable as containing a clause which suspended its ratification for a year, the intention being to give the Pope the opportunity of yielding by his own action. But this not being done, the Act was ratified by the King's letters patent and confirmed in 1534. In 1533 anti-Papal legislation was continued, and produced the famous Statute for Restraint of Appeals, the best known and most frequently quoted of all the Reformation statutes. Its preamble set forth in most emphatic language the independence and nationality of the Church of England, and the power and right of the spiritualty in it 'to determine all doubts within the kingdom;' and it enacts that all spiritual causes were to be determined by the Church courts in England, without appeal to Rome being allowed or Roman prohibitions regarded. Appeals were to lie from the archdeacon to the bishop, from the bishop to the archbishop, and (in the case of the King and his heirs) from the archbishop to the Upper House of Convocation. This arrangement was afterwards somewhat altered by a provision for an appeal from the Archbishop's court to the King in Chancery, the cause to be heard by a body of delegates to be nominated by the King. Papal interference with the election to bishoprics was forbidden, and it was enacted that the Crown should send a license to the chapter (*congé d'eslire*) to elect, and that this license should be accompanied by a letter missive specifying the person to be elected, under the penalties of *Præmunire* for refusal. Papal dispensations were

REFORMATION PARLIAMENT AND CONVOCATION 17

abolished, and the archbishops were to have the right of granting them in certain cases. The King was invested with visitatorial power over all monasteries, colleges, &c. This Act declared 'that the King and Parliament did not intend to decline or vary from the congregation of Christ's Church in anything concerning the very articles of the catholic faith of Christendom, and in any other things declared by Scripture and the Word of God necessary for salvation.' What these things were, however, was as it seems, to be left to the King's own judgment; for the King was left absolutely free 'to visit, repress, redress, reform, order, correct, restrain, and amend all such errors, *heresies*, abuses, contempts, and enormities, whatsoever they be, *which by any manner of spiritual jurisdiction ought and may be lawfully reformed.*' The firstfruits and tenths, formerly paid to the Pope, were also now conferred upon the King.

Visitatorial rights given to the Crown

Supremacy Act

Firstfruits and tenths given to the King

Thus a complete transformation in the relations of the clergy to the Crown had been effected. The clergy, surprised, confounded, and intimidated by the King's vigour, and having no love for the Papal system, under which they had long groaned, opposed no effectual opposition to any of these drastic measures, and in their Convocations advanced in parallel lines with the action of Parliament. They voted the Royal Supremacy under the fear of the penalties of the Præmunire Statute. In 1533 both Convocations voted that the marriage of Henry with Catherine was illegal, and could not be dispensed with by the Pope. In 1534 both Convocations, in like manner,

Vote of the clergy against the jurisdiction of the Pope

voted 'that the Roman bishop has no greater jurisdiction given him by God in this kingdom than any other bishop.' This was also voted by the two Universities, by the clergy of each diocese by means of forms sent round by the bishops through the archdeacons, by all the most considerable abbots and their monks, and by all public lay bodies. By the end of 1534, therefore, the renunciation of the Papal authority in England both by clergy and laity was complete. This was followed up (1535) by the King's proclamation of his style and title—'in terrâ supremum caput Anglicanæ ecclesiæ'—and by a proclamation (June 9) for the abrogation of the usurped authority of the Pope, and for the erasure of his name from all the service books.

CHAPTER III.

THE ADVOCATES OF REFORMATION.

THE Parliament of 1529 was doubtless very subservient to the will of the King, but it would hardly have passed with such readiness so many Acts involving almost a revolution in the ecclesiastical status, had there not been in the country a growing desire for change. It might be thought, indeed, that the increase of this reforming spirit would influence the spiritual peers in the House of Lords rather to resist change than to welcome it. With them, however, it is probable that another motive prevailed. They thought that the best way of securing

General desire for change in the religious status

safety for the Church, and keeping the King interested in its defence, was to aid him in his attacks on the Papal system, which from time immemorial had been a miserable yoke on the neck of all English prelates, but which, partly from *esprit de corps*, partly from fear of the power of Rome, they had felt constrained to defend. Now there was a happy opportunity of shaking themselves free and at the same time of obliging the King, of whose autocratic temper and unscrupulous readiness to act they had a wholesome dread. This may account for the fact that all the bishops, with the sole exception of Fisher, went with the King in the divorce case, and that no vigorous protest, no effectual opposition, appears to have been raised in the Upper House against any of the Bills taking away the Papal authority. But while the bishops may have acted with a view of pleasing the King, and of keeping him faithful to the Church system, there is no doubt that the Commons and lay peers were urged on by a strong stimulus from without. The Duke of Norfolk writes to the ambassador at Rome, ' This realm did never grudge the tenth part against the abuses of the Church, at no Parliament in my days, as they do now.'

Who were the promoters of this spirit? Cambridge seems to have been the chief nurse of the teachers of Reforming views. It was from that University that the knot of Lutherans was brought by Wolsey (whether designedly or not) to his new college at Oxford. Several of these men were conspicuous afterwards. At Cambridge Mr. Stafford, who seems to have owed his love of the Scriptures to Dean Colet, lectured on Holy Scripture, freely

<small>Cambridge Reformers</small>

condemning many of the superstitions of the day. By Stafford Thomas Bilney was impressed, and by Bilney Hugh Latimer. As regards Bilney he never varied, according to Foxe, from the views on the Sacrament of the altar held by 'the grossest Catholics;' but he condemned pilgrimages, and the worship of saints and relics, and for this he was judged a heretic by Bishop Tonstal and made to carry a fagot at Paul's Cross. Afterwards he recanted his recantation and was burned by Bishop Nix at Norwich (1531).

Hugh Latimer, the son of a Leicestershire farmer, was, up to the taking his Bachelor of Divinity degree, a zealous upholder of the old superstitions. He then fell under the influence of Bilney and adopted a considerable change in his religious sentiments. His terse and witty style of preaching attracted much attention at Cambridge and brought the Bishop of Ely to listen to one of his sermons. Latimer, seeing the entrance of the Bishop, turned his discourse to a description of what a Christian prelate should be. The Bishop, perhaps not much soothed by the admonition, required Latimer after the conclusion of the sermon to declare against the errors of Martin Luther; but to this he objected. He then inhibited him from preaching; but Latimer continued to preach in the exempt church of the Austin Friars, whose prior, Dr. Barnes, was a favourer of Lutheran views. An information laid against him by the Bishop and the Cambridge doctors now brought Latimer before Cardinal Wolsey. The Cardinal found him well versed in school divinity, and having heard the substance of the sermon delivered by him before the Bishop of Ely, saw nothing to disapprove, and gave Latimer a general license to preach throughout England. The King's physician, Dr. Butts, who had been sent to Cambridge to influence the University about the divorce matter, seems to have been the means of bringing Latimer to preach at Court. The King liked his plain speaking, and liked him all the better because the Cambridge vice-chancellor, Dr. Buckmaster, who was opposed to the divorce and who was among the audience, showed his dislike of his doctrine. The beginning of Sir T. More's Chancellorship (1529) was marked by a violent proclamation against heretical books. This does not appear to have produced the required effect; so another proclamation, of a milder type, came out, which, while it condemns heretical books, promises that, when they are cleared away, the King will cause the Scripture to be translated into English by 'great, learned, and Catholic persons.' Upon this proclamation Latimer wrote the King a long letter to encourage him in his design of having the Scripture translated, and offering some apology for those who circulated the forbidden books. The character of this letter would be higher were there not to be found in it a sharp cut at the Cardinal, to whom Latimer owed so much, and who was just then under the royal displeasure. Latimer was now promoted to the living of West Kington in Wiltshire, which he owed to the patronage of Thomas Crumwell. Soon he was in trouble for his preaching, articles having been exhibited against him in Convocation in 1532. He at first refused the paper tendered to him for subscription, then accepted it, and then again preached in opposition to it. Perhaps he held the dangerous

His letter to the King

doctrine that the obligation to preach 'the truth' is superior to promises. His zeal caused him to be regarded by Crumwell as a valuable instrument for furthering the Reformation, and in 1535 he was made Bishop of Worcester.

Made Bishop of Worcester

It has been said that while Latimer was at Cambridge a church was lent him by Dr. Barnes, Prior of the Austin Friars. Barnes was one of the first men in England in trouble for Lutheranism. In 1521, at the book-burning at St. Paul's, he was obliged to throw a fagot into the flames, to signify that this might well have been his own fate. This, however, does not appear to have driven him from his convictions. He was held to have relapsed, it may be on account of his support of Latimer, and escaping, carried on from abroad a controversy with Sir Thomas More as to the nature of the true Church, which he held to be invisible.

Dr. Barnes

A more notable man than Barnes was John Fryth, who had been a member of the Cardinal's college. Being suspected of heresy, he fled from England and joined Tyndale in Germany. When More, Fisher, and Rastall endeavoured to defend the doctrine of Purgatory, Fryth, having obtained their treatises, proceeded to demolish them with much skill and learning. His end was very tragical. He was the victim of treachery, and shamefully condemned to death by the bishops. Having returned to England, he was arrested and thrown into prison, and, when there, was entrapped by a pretended convert to write something on the Eucharist. This fell into Sir T. More's hands, and was the cause of bringing Fryth before Bishops Stokes-

John Fryth

ley, Longland, and Gardiner. Fryth spoke with remarkable moderation, and made no absolute objection to anything but the worship of the elements. This, however, was sufficient to condemn him to the stake. Archbishop Cranmer had an interview with him, but left him unconvinced and as fitting fuel for the flames. The startling brutality of this sentence led to a change of the law touching heretics. An Act was passed which prohibited the bishops from acting on mere suspicion, and required the testimony of two witnesses and a trial in open court. Considering the fearful danger ever menacing them from the law, it is marvellous to find so many men ready to advocate these perilous opinions.

Yet Sir Thomas More, who acted as a general champion of the old superstitions, had a whole host of disputants to contend with. Of these none gave him more trouble than William Tyndale, whom he attacked in his 'Dialogue.' Tyndale answered by a lengthy Reply. Then there came a 'Confutation,' and an answer to the Confutation, with much railing language on the part of More and some very feeble arguments from Tyndale. The opinions which Tyndale advocated were those of Zwingli. He held the Eucharist to be designed for a 'lively memorial,' or, in other words, to 'preach,' and his doctrine on the connection of faith and works seemed dangerously Antinomian. But it is not on his controversial works that Tyndale's fame rests. By his admirable translation of the New Testament he conferred a greater benefit on the Church and gave a greater stimulus to the Reformation than perhaps any other man. The translation of Wycliffe and Purvey

William Tyndale

His translation of the New Testament

had never been printed, and existed only in a few imperfect manuscripts. Its English also was obsolete and hardly intelligible to the men of the sixteenth century. Tyndale was a good scholar, having studied both at Oxford and Cambridge, and he had the advantage of the edition of the Greek Testament, with a Latin version published by Erasmus in 1516. He determined to translate from the original Greek, and with the help of friends, he brought out at Worms two editions of the New Testament in English in the year 1526. It has been already stated how sedulous the bishops were in burning these books, and Sir Thomas More and others were no less eager in denouncing the translation as imperfect and erroneous. Its merits, however, were too solid to be affected by ignorant abuse, and it finally triumphed by becoming the foundation of the Authorised Version of 1611. It is sad to note that Tyndale, like Fryth, was brought by treachery to a cruel death, being strangled and burned in Germany at the instance of the King of England, in 1536.

Archbishop Cranmer can hardly as yet be counted as one of the advocates of Reformation in religion. He owed his promotion to his zeal in the divorce case, in which he became one of the principal agents after the fall of Wolsey, and to finish which he was raised to the Primacy (March 30, 1533) on the death of Warham. He pronounced the sentence of divorce between Henry and Catherine (May 23, 1533), and took a ready part in the anti-Papal movement, but in his religious views he was still unchanged, and could see Fryth handed over to the secular arm without an attempt to save him.

A more decided and earnest partisan of the movement (to whom, indeed, it owed much of its force and vigour) was Thomas Crumwell. Crumwell had risen from quite a low station by the dexterity which he displayed in the service of Cardinal Wolsey. He had loyally defended the Cardinal on his disgrace, and had thus recommended himself to the King, whose principal adviser he soon became. Staking his political career on the success of the Reformation movement, Crumwell omitted nothing to advance it. Doubtless he was the author of some of the legislative Acts which ensured the freedom of the Church of England from Rome. It was Crumwell who carefully devised the scheme for influencing public opinion on the matter of the Royal Supremacy. Justices of the peace and all public officers were to be enlisted in the work, while the bishops were not only to procure from their clergy the renunciation of the Papal supremacy, but were also to take care that the name and title of the Bishop of Rome should be expunged from all prayers, rubrics, and canons, and specially from the great 'sentence of curse' against the enemies of Holy Church wont to be recited four times a year in churches.

Thomas Crumwell

When the Nun of Kent, Elizabeth Barton, who was supposed to have visions and revelations, was being made use of by the Roman party to check the anti-Papal movement, and was put in communication with Sir Thomas More and Bishop Fisher, the two great champions of the old state of things, Crumwell saw his opportunity for ruining his chief opponents. More had still sufficient influence

Affair of the Nun of Kent

with the King to keep his name out of the bill of attainder. He had, in fact, in no way encouraged the nun's revelations. But Bishop Fisher was found guilty of misprision of treason, and compounded for a fine of 300*l*. This partial success against the two leading men of the old party was not, however, sufficient for Crumwell. The Act of Succession, passed in 1534, was drawn in such terms that it involved a rejection of the Pope as well as a promise to be faithful to the children of Queen Anne. This Act was to be confirmed by an oath, which Crumwell knew well neither More nor Fisher could take. They were willing to accept the succession, but not the wording of the Act. An attempt made by Cranmer to allow them this modified acceptance was opposed by Crumwell, sufficiently indicating his set purpose to destroy them.

The oath in the Succession Act

More and Fisher were committed to the Tower, and when Parliament met in the autumn of 1534, an elaborate scheme was carried out by the King and Crumwell for their destruction. An Act was passed giving a legal sanction to the wording of the oath, which had not been included in the first Act; and a second Act followed, which is one of the most atrocious that was ever put upon the Statute Book of England. This Act, generally known as the Treason Act, made it high treason to speak against any of the King's titles or prerogatives (including the Supremacy), or even to *imagine* anything against them. Persons were to be held guilty of treason who would not *in words* assent to the Royal Supremacy. 'Malicious silence' was to be a sufficient condemnation. It was

Condemnation of More and Fisher

thus deliberately attempted to cause the forfeit of a man's life for his thoughts. It cannot be supposed that the King would have assented to such a murderous law as this had he not been specially exasperated by the Pope's action in annulling Cranmer's sentence of divorce (thus making Anne's daughter illegitimate) and declaring his intention to excommunicate Henry. His fury against the Pope found expression in this violent demonstration against his adherents, suggested probably by Crumwell, and passed by a too subservient Parliament. Under this law the Carthusian monks in London —men famed for their piety and devotion—were ruthlessly put to death ; and the witty and upright ex-Chancellor, Sir Thomas More, and the venerable Bishop Fisher, having been brought to trial in Westminster Hall, and condemned, both for 'malicious silence' and for words said to have been uttered in derogation of the Supremacy, were beheaded (June 22 and July 6, 1535). While Fisher was lying in prison the Pope had sent him the gift of a cardinal's hat, an honour which served still further to exasperate the King against him. The horror caused by the judicial murder of two such men as More and Fisher could not easily be suppressed, and it needed all Crumwell's skill to meet and check the tide of indignation which was rising both at home and abroad. Ambassadors were sent to all the foreign courts to explain, and at home a circular was sent to the justices of the peace (a favourite device of Crumwell's) bidding them to see that the clergy published *four times a year* an account of the 'treasons' of the late Bishop of Rochester and Sir Thomas More.

The Court divines were also set to work with the pen. Dr. Sampson, Dean of the Chapel Royal, composed a Latin oration in support of the Royal Supremacy; Bishop Gardiner wrote a book on 'True Obedience' (1535), which was re-edited the next year by Bonner, then Archdeacon of Leicester, with a laudatory preface. But Crumwell was far from depending for the success of his policy in carrying forward the Reformation on the somewhat hollow support of divines who wrote to order. He desired to enlist the mass of the nation in the work of Reformation, and to force the King's hand, who had no wish for any religious changes, but only cared about the establishment of his own autocracy. With this view Crumwell had long been secretly preparing for the publication of the whole Bible in English. Tyndale's Testament had been proscribed, but the King had committed himself to a promise that an English translation should be made; Cranmer had urged the necessity of this in the Convocation of 1534, and some beginning had been effected. This about coincided with the *completion* of an English translation of the Old and New Testaments from the Vulgate, which Crumwell had procured to be made in Germany. The scholar employed by him was Miles Coverdale, who had been an Austin Friar in the house at Cambridge over which Robert Barnes presided, had adopted Lutheran views, and had fled abroad. The work was finished and printed by October 1535, was published in England without express royal sanction, and spread rapidly. Probably it owed its toleration to the fact that it was a translation from the Vulgate, and made no attempt to give a new rendering of the original. The same year which witnessed the publication of the first English Bible witnessed also the printing of the first Reforming Primer. This book contained a condemnation of saint and image worship and of superstitious legends and practices, furnished some good prayers for private use, and was altogether of a distinctly Reforming type.

First Reforming Primer

While Crumwell was thus skilfully striving to leaven the people with Reforming views, with the King he remained in greater favour than ever. The climax was reached when, in 1535, there was issued under the Great Seal an instrument empowering Crumwell to use to its full extent the Royal Supremacy as it was set forth in the Act of Parliament—that is, to have a complete, absolute, irresponsible power over all ecclesiastical persons, corporations, laws; to inflict any censures or punishments which he pleased; to ' deal in any way with the ecclesiastical property; to preside at and direct the elections of prelates, confirm those rightly made and annul the contrary; to institute and induct into possession of churches.' To make this more than Papal power the more effective the jurisdiction of all bishops was suspended, and then restored to them under the royal license, so that they became the officers of the Vicar-General; and Crumwell's deputies being endowed with the same power as himself, the ecclesiastical system was for the time completely in abeyance, and the Church had exchanged the tyranny of Rome for a tyranny nearer, more searching, more drastic, and more dangerous. As it happened, no special damage accrued to the Church from this extravagant exaggeration of

Crumwell appointed Vicar-General

the royal supremacy. No bishops were appointed simply by royal warrant without consecration, no laymen were commissioned to administer the Sacraments or to preach, and the attention of the King and Crumwell was soon drawn away from ecclesiastical schemes to the more congenial task of plundering and suppressing the monasteries. This was a policy suggested to Crumwell by his previous experience with Cardinal Wolsey, and it was a bribe to the King to continue his favour to him—so enormous that during its progress, and while he still was necessary for carrying it on, he felt himself secure of the royal approbation whatever schemes he might entertain. We now proceed to consider this crowning act of the 'Reformation Parliament,' which has drawn upon it laudation from some, but unmeasured abuse from others.

CHAPTER IV.

FALL OF THE MONASTERIES.
1536-1539.

FOR some time before the reign of Henry VIII. the whole nation had come to the conclusion that monasteries had Decay of the outlived their day. For more than a century monasteries very few had been founded, and the entire relaxation of the rules, and the general mixing of monks in secular affairs, showed that the members of the monastic houses were themselves of the same opinion. It is sometimes contended that monasteries were very valuable for the alms they distributed; but, as the houses were mostly apart from the centres of population, and their annals show but little traces of any thoughtful charity, this can hardly be estimated of any great value. And while the monasteries could plead no special ground for continued preservation, their very considerable estates were a constant temptation to the spoiler. These estates had often been grievously mismanaged, and in many instances fraudulently alienated. The houses were almost universally deeply in debt, and there seemed nothing to check a strong and vigorous interference with this mass of misapplied property, save the religious sentiment of the rulers and the strong protection of Rome. When the King and Parliament and the whole Church of England formally broke with Rome it is evident that the great monastic institutions of the land were in imminent danger. The Pope himself had shown the way to their suppression. Besides various authorised suppressions sanctioned in earlier days, the Bulls granted to Wolsey had given into his hands a considerable number of monastic houses, the property of which had been dealt with by Crumwell, who was thus a ready-prepared instrument for more general spoliation.

The opportunity was given to Crumwell to buy the favour of the King by a monstrous bribe, and he did *Their suppression resolved upon* not hesitate to avail himself of it. Henry did not need much persuasion to use this ready method of replenishing his exhausted exchequer. The suppression of the monasteries was resolved upon. There would not have been so much occasion to find fault with this resolve had it been carried out in a different way. A well-considered Act of Parliament, with full regard for life interests, a judicious application of the funds, and a fitting use found for the consecrated buildings, might have done much to excuse it in the judgment of posterity. But, unhappily, it was thought necessary, in deference to the religious sentiment of the nation, to endeavour to ground the suppression on the plea of morality and necessary correction of abuses; and hence a mass of slanderous and unproved charges was got together by a body of visitors appointed by Crumwell, and was laid before Parliament to ensure the passing of the Act.[1]

The passing of the Act The first Act of Suppression was passed in February 1536. In the House of Lords the mitred abbots, who formed a large part of that body, offered no opposition, inasmuch as the Act only decreed the confiscation of houses with a revenue under 200*l.* a year. This selfish spirit—a natural product of the monastic system—did not avail long to save those who were thus ready to sacrifice their weaker brethren. The bishops also readily accepted the confiscation. Monasteries had always been thorns in their sides. Defying, eluding, or resisting their visitations, ever striving for

[1] The original indictment against the monasteries, called the 'Black Book,' has been destroyed or lost. There remain in the Record Office certain documents called 'Comperta,' which are a sort of tabulated statement of the immoralities imputed to religious persons and their houses. These cannot be regarded as historically reliable; but to find sufficient evidence against the purity and discipline of the 'religious' we need not travel beyond the bishops' registers, the entries in which are above suspicion, and which go far to substantiate some of the worst accusations. No doubt plenty of scandals might be alleged with truth, but why allege them? This was a cruel method of carrying out a predetermined policy.

FALL OF THE MONASTERIES

an *imperium in imperio*, systematically robbing parish churches, and always ready with the appeal to Rome, the monasteries were little loved by them, and were abandoned to their fate with complacency.

After the passing of the Act, Commissioners were sent to the smaller monasteries to take inventories, to settle the pensions of the monks and nuns if they should desire to enter secular life, or to arrange for their being transferred to one of the larger monasteries still left intact ; also to report upon the buildings — whether the churches should be pulled down for the sake of the lead and bells—and generally to arrange for the demolition of the house. These Commissioners reported to a Court called the Court of Augmentation, which was specially appointed to consider and arrange all the matter of the suppression and to receive the spoil, and which, when the procedure had been determined upon from the report of the Commissioners, sent receivers to carry out the sale and demolition of the monastic property. The monasteries suppressed under the first Act amounted in number to 376, and produced a revenue of about 32,000*l.* to the Crown, and a capital sum of about 100,000*l.* arising from the plate and valuables. The demolition of all these ancient buildings and the ejection of their inmates were equivalent to a social revolution, as the monks were great employers of labour, and were frequently attended by a host of servants. Yet in all the southern parts of the land there does not appear to have been any opposition or disturbance created by the demolition. The thing principally noted is the eagerness of the people to steal the goods of the condemned house. In fact, the

Commissioners to arrange for the demolition

monastic chronicles generally represent the religious house as being on very bad terms with its neighbours.

In the north things were different. Here some active spirits among the religious were able to incite the people to join with them in open revolt. But it is very observable that the grievances which were alleged as a justification for the 'Pilgrimage of Grace' were by no means confined to the suppression of the monasteries. The people were equally, if not more, excited by the 'Statute of Uses,' which affected the transfer of property; by the heavy imposts which they had to bear; by the counsellors 'of mean birth' whom the King had about him, and by the danger which they thought menaced the plate and valuables of the parish churches. The rebellion assumed most formidable proportions both in Lincolnshire and Yorkshire, and the King was obliged to make long explanations of his policy, and to promise considerable concessions before it could be overcome.

The Pilgrimage of Grace

Far from benefiting the cause of the monastic houses, the immediate effect of the Pilgrimage of Grace was to bring ruin on those monasteries which had as yet been spared. For their complicity or alleged complicity in it, twelve abbots were hanged, drawn, and quartered, and their houses were seized by the Crown. Every means was employed by a new set of Commissioners to bring about the surrender of others of the greater abbeys. The houses were visited, and their pretended relics and various tricks to encourage the devotion of the people were exposed. Surrenders went rapidly on during the years 1537 and 1538, and it became necessary to obtain a new Act of

Disastrous effect on greater monasteries

FALL OF THE MONASTERIES

Parliament to vest the property of the later surrenders in the Crown. Eager to grasp the whole of the spoil which now seemed within his reach, the King sanctioned acts of grievous and revolting injustice against the abbots of the greater abbeys. Of these none made so great an impression at the time, and has been so well remembered by posterity, as the murder of Abbot Whiting of Glastonbury, on the pretence of treason in having concealed the goods belonging to the house. This poor man had often bribed and flattered Crumwell, but found no help from him in his hour of need. Nothing, indeed, can be more tragical than the way in which the greater abbeys were destroyed on manufactured charges and for imaginary crimes. These houses had been described in the first Act of Parliament as 'great and honourable,' wherein 'religion was right well kept and observed.' Yet now they were pitilessly destroyed.

Cruelties of the Dissolution.

A revenue of about 131,607*l.* is computed to have thus come to the Crown, while the movables are valued at 400,000*l.* How was this vast sum of money expended? (1) By the Act for the suppression of the greater monasteries the King was empowered to erect six new sees with their deans and chapters, namely, Westminster, Oxford, Chester, Gloucester, Bristol, and Peterborough. He had formerly, in Wolsey's time, contemplated a larger number, but his views were not the same under the influence of the Cardinal and that of Thomas Crumwell. (2) Some monasteries were turned into collegiate churches, and many of the abbey churches, after the destruction of the conventual buildings, were assigned

Amount of spoil obtained. Its appropriation

as parish churches for the use of the people. (3) Some grammar schools were erected. (4) A considerable sum is said to have been spent in making roads and in fortifying the coasts of the Channel. (5) But by far the greater part of the monastic property passed into the hands of the nobility and gentry, either by purchase at very easy rates, or by direct gift from the Crown. This was the policy of Crumwell, who astutely foresaw that the great change which had been effected would be made perpetual in its effects, if all the leading men of the country were directly and personally interested in maintaining it. Henry was not of a parsimonious character like his father, but rather inclined to profuse extravagance, and readily parted with his new acquisitions. Hallam is of opinion that this disposition of the conventual estates, 'however illaudable in its motive, has proved upon the whole more beneficial to England than any other disposition would have turned out.'

Transfer of the abbey lands to laymen

There were, however, two manifest evils which flowed directly from it. The first was the creation of a great mass of lay tithes—an absurd anomaly, and a grievous injustice to the clergy. Throughout all their history the monasteries had been eager to get impropriations of tithes, and to reduce the parish priest to the miserable stipend paid for a vicar. Now the tithes which they had filched from the Church, instead of being restored to the clergy, were greedily seized by lay hands. 'The impropriations, says Hallam, 'were in no instance, I believe, restored to the parochial clergy.' Thus, secondly, the poverty of the clergy was not only continued, but was griev-

Evils resulting from this

ously increased. While the monasteries lasted, the vicar who served the parish church was often a member of the corporate body; in the case of Houses of Canons, who were all in orders, almost universally so. The smallness of the vicarial stipend did not, therefore, much affect him. But when, on the Dissolution, this alone formed the support of the priest, the greatest inconvenience followed, even if it were regularly paid. But there is ample testimony that in a great many cases, when the tithes passed into lay hands, the vicarial stipend was not paid at all. Hence followed an utter cessation of the offices in many churches, and a legacy of trouble and poverty was bequeathed to the Church for all time. Henry's ecclesiastical spoliations were

Act to give the King chantry and collegiate property completed by the Act passed in 1545, which gave the King the property of all colleges, free chapels, chantries, hospitals, fraternities, guilds, which were to be dealt with by the Court of Augmentation. This Act was renewed in the next reign, but its terribly sweeping provisions were never fully carried out.

The monks and nuns ejected from the monasteries had small pensions assigned to them, which are said to *Hard case of the ejected monks and nuns* have been regularly paid; but to many of them the sudden return into a world with which they had become utterly unacquainted, and in which they had no part to play, was a terrible hardship. This hardship was greatly increased by the Six Article Law, which enacted that vows of chastity, once taken, must be rigidly observed and made the marriage of the secularised 'religious' illegal under heavy penalties.

During the latter years of the reign of Henry VIII. the attention is drawn aside to the fearful parodies of justice; to the execution, at the same time and place, of one set of persons for denying the Supremacy, of another for Lutheran heresy (1540);[1] to the murder of the venerable Countess of Salisbury in revenge for the sharp words of her son, Cardinal Pole (1541); to the torture and burning of a delicate and learned lady (Anne Ayscough) for alleged heresy on the Eucharist (1546); and we are apt to forget what the miseries of the poor ejected monks and nuns must have been in that harsh and troubled time.

We turn with pleasure from the destructive and vindictive policy of this reign, from the savage blows and repulsive cruelties which marked the extinction of the old ecclesiastical system, to the consideration of the constructive process which, during all these horrors, was steadily proceeding, and paving the way for a happier state of things in the future.

---

[1] On the same day Abel, Featherstone, and Powel, priests, and doctors of divinity, and Barnes, Gerard, and Jerome, Lutherans, who had been *attainted in Parliament* for heresies, 'the number of which was too long to be repeated,' were burned. It is calculated that sixty-five persons were executed in Henry's reign for denying the Supremacy, and sixty-one were condemned but not executed. The number of those executed for heresy was also very considerable.

CHAPTER V.

RELIGIOUS PROGRESS DURING THE REIGN OF HENRY VIII.

1536–1547.

SINCE the days of St. Osmund of Salisbury, who about 1085 put forth his *Custom Book*, containing a revised edition of the offices of the English Church, but little had been done by the Church of England as a body to instruct or enlighten the clergy or the people. The old fables still remained in the Breviary, occupying a position of equal honour with the words of Scripture, and everything was in a language 'not understanded of the people.' The idea of a religious service was that the people should assemble in church and say their own prayers, while the Mass was being celebrated in an unknown tongue, their part in the service being confined to occasionally exhibiting respect for what was going on by standing or genuflecting. To provide them with prayers to say at this time there were divers Primers, Manuals, Hours, and little books, containing English prayers or doggerel explanations of the various parts of the Mass. There were also many poems in doggerel verse, both French and English, recounting the chief facts of Scripture; but in spite of such useful little books, and in spite of Wycliffe's English version of the Bible, and his pungent English Tracts, it is hardly possible to exaggerate the state of ignorance concerning religious truth in which the people of England were at the beginning of the sixteenth century.

<small>The ancient Church services</small>

<small>Ignorance of the people</small>

This ignorance was compulsory, and not patiently accepted by the people themselves. The bishops were anxious to keep them from knowledge, from fear lest this knowledge should produce heresy. Instead of providing useful instruction, their policy was to debar the people from all instruction.[1] But when books were to be had, repressive measures could not prevent their being bought and read. The little English books attacking the Church system, which were printed abroad, were imported into England in great numbers, and were eagerly bought. Tyndale's Testaments were purchased in large quantities at a price equivalent to two weeks' wages of a labourer. In the Convocation of 1534 a portentous list of heretical books was handed by the Lower House to the Upper. The King and the bishops saw that they must accept the situation, and provide some instruction for the people, who would no longer be denied. Hence the promise in 1530 that the Bible should be translated into English. Hence Cranmer's movement in Convocation in 1534, and the attempt to arrange translators. Hence Crumwell's more decided action, which produced the English Bible of 1535. But the publication of the text of the Bible was not sufficient. How were the ignorant people to formulate their doctrines rightly when nothing was done for them by the clergy, their proper instructors? When the Convocation of Canterbury met in 1536, Bishop Latimer preached the sermon, *ad clerum*. His discourse was a very remark-

[1] In the fifteenth century Bishop Pecock's principal offence was his having written theological books in English. In the Register of Bishop Chedworth, at the same period, men are censured for having books in English, without reference to the contents of the books.

able one. He denounced with withering scorn the old superstitions as to image-worship and purgatory, and represented God as addressing the clergy. 'You teach your own traditions and seek your own glory and profit. You preach very seldom, and when you do preach, do nothing but cumber them that preach truly, as much as lieth in you. I would that Christian people should hear my doctrine, and at their convenient leisure read it also, as many as would. Your care is not that all men may hear it, but all your care is that no layman do read it.' When such plain words could be addressed to the assembled clergy by a bishop enjoying royal favour, it is clear that the time of enforced ignorance was drawing to a close.

Bishop Latimer's sermon to the Convocation

The first attempt to put out anything like an authoritative manual of instruction was made by the publication of the 'Ten Articles' in 1536. The first draft of these articles is in the King's hand, but he no doubt had the assistance of some of the bishops in drawing them up. They are borrowed chiefly from the Confession of Augsburg. They begin by stating that the Scriptures are to be taken as the rule of faith, as interpreted by the Three Creeds and the 'four holy Councils.' They treat, first of Baptism, which is declared to be necessary for the remission of sins. Then of Penance, 'a thing so necessary for man's salvation, that no man which after his baptism is fallen again, and hath committed deadly sin, can without the same be saved or attain everlasting life.' It consists in contrition, confession, and amendment. As to confession, all are bid 'in nowise to contemn the auricular confession made unto the ministers of the Church, but to repute the same as a very expedient

The Ten Articles

and necessary mean whereby they may require and ask absolution at the priest's hands;' and that 'they ought and must give no less faith and credence to the words of absolution pronounced by the ministers of the Church than they would unto the very words and voice of God Himself.' Amendment of life is also necessary, and the bringing forth fruits of faith in good living. As regards the Sacrament of the Altar, men are to believe that 'under the form and figure of bread and wine, which we there presently do see and perceive by outward senses, is verily, substantially, and really contained and comprehended the very selfsame body and blood of our Saviour Jesus Christ, which was born of the Virgin Mary, and suffered on the cross for our redemption, which is corporally, really, and in the very substance, exhibited, distributed, and received unto and of all them which receive the said sacrament,' and therefore due reverence and fitting preparation are to be used for that sacrament. Justification, or remission of sins, is obtained by contrition and faith joined with charity, the only meritorious cause being the merits of Jesus Christ. Images may be used as 'representers of virtue and good example,' but 'as for censing them, kneeling and offering unto them, with other like worshippings, although the same hath entered by devotion and fallen to custom, yet the people are to be taught that they in nowise do it, nor think it meet to be done to the same images, but only to be done to God.' Saints are to be honoured, ' but not with that confidence and honour which are only due to God, trusting to attain at their hands that which must be had only of God.' They may be prayed to as intercessors to God for us, ' so that it be done without any vain superstition as to think that any saint will hear us sooner than Christ, or that any saint doth serve for one thing more than another, or is patron of the same.' The rites and ceremonies of the Church are 'not to be contemned and cast away, but to be used and continued as things good and laudable, but none of these ceremonies have power to remit sin.' As regards Purgatory, it is good and charitable to pray for Christian souls, and to have Masses for them, but 'forasmuch as the place where they be, the name thereof, and kind of pains there also be to us uncertain by Scripture, therefore this with all other things we remit to Almighty God, unto whose mercy it is meet and convenient for us to commend them; but it is so much necessary that such abuses be clearly put away, which under the name of *purgatory* hath been advanced as to make men believe that through the Bishop of Rome's pardons souls might be clearly delivered out of purgatory, and all the pains of it; or that Masses said at Scala Cœli, or otherwise in any place, or before any image, might likewise deliver them from all their pain, and send them straight to Heaven, and other like abuses.'

These Articles, originally drafted by the King and some of the more reforming bishops, were accepted by the Convocation of Canterbury, and signed by all the members of it. They were also accepted by the Archbishop of York and the Bishop of Durham for the northern Convocation. At the head of the signatures appears that of Thomas Crumwell, who, as the Vicar-General of the King, claimed to take precedence of all the bishops. The Articles are very remarkable, as representing the immense progress which had been made since the time when the King wrote in defence of the 'Seven Sacraments,' and Bishop Fisher and Sir Thomas More in defence of the doctrine of Purgatory. Of the seven so-called sacraments, four are entirely omitted in these Articles, the doctrine of Purgatory is practically abandoned, and the teaching on the Eucharist, which omits the crucial words 'that bread and wine no longer remain,' represents rather the consubstantiation theory of the Lutherans than the transubstantiation of the Church. The influences of Crumwell and of the German theology are here very evident. The document was in many ways extremely well calculated for the guidance of the clergy in the instruction of the people.

Doubtless political causes had much to do in giving their special character to the Ten Articles. Henry, though strongly pressed, had refused to accept the Confession of Augsburg or to join the Smalcald League. At the same time he was bitterly incensed against the new Pope, Paul III., who, as he knew, had excommunicated him, and was only kept back from the publication of the sentence by the influence of the King of France. While, therefore, he was not prepared to make common cause with the German Reformers, he was also desirous to show to the Roman party that he was ready to accept a definite position for the Church of England on the basis of a national confession of faith. The clergy, readily following the King's lead, voted that whereas a true General Council ought in all things to be obeyed, the Council now summoned by the Pope, 'not christianly nor charitably, but for and upon private malice and ambition, or other worldly and carnal respects,' ought to be treated with contempt.

Protest against proposed Council of Mantua

This Convocation also voted the diminution of the number of saints' days and holy days, and that all the dedication feasts of churches should be observed on a uniform day, viz. the first Sunday in October. The Convocation was dissolved in July, 1536, and soon afterwards was published the first set of 'Royal Injunctions' to the clergy, enforcing upon their attention not only the 'Ten Articles' and the new rules about holy days, but also divers other regulations which do not appear to have been before Convocation, and which, therefore, were due to that theory of the Royal Supremacy which the King had adopted.

Diminution of holy days

First 'Royal Injunctions'

In the autumn of this year the breaking out of the northern rebellion, known as the 'Pilgrimage of Grace,' and the voting by an irregular assembly of clergy at York of a series of propositions directly contradicting the 'Ten Articles,' and upholding all the old superstitions, made it necessary to take some further steps to influence the people. The bishops were directed to distribute copies of the Articles, and to explain that in them there was no departure from the Catholic religion. They were also to teach the people that the 'honest ceremonies' of the Church were by all means to be upheld.

Measures taken to influence the people

Crumwell, however, perceived that something more was needed for the instruction of the people and the confirmation of the Reformation movement. The Ten Articles were a good foundation, but they left the actual instruction in the hands of the clergy, and it did not as yet appear that the clergy had any disposition to perform this duty.

The making of the book, 'The Institution of a Christian Man'

Crumwell accordingly got together a meeting of the bishops in the early part of the following year, with the object of discussing the plan of a work of more full instruction. An account of this meeting is given in a letter of Mr. Aless, a Scot, who was brought in by Crumwell with the view of upholding his plans. Some of the bishops made considerable objections; but these were overruled, and a large committee of divines was appointed to draw up a complete manual of faith and morals. This committee worked with great diligence, separate portions of the subject being entrusted to each member; so that it produced in a very short time the book known as 'The Institution of a Christian Man,' which was signed by the King, and printed and published in May, 1537. The book is divided into four parts. The first contains the exposition of the Creed; the second that of the Sacraments—which are here seven, and not three as in the 'Ten Articles'; the third, the exposition of the Ten Commandments; the fourth, that of the Lord's Prayer and the Ave, with articles on Justification and Purgatory. The Ten Articles are embodied in the book almost verbatim. The book is a very remarkable one in many ways. It shows great power of theological disquisition and of practical exhortation. Some of its enunciations are so happy and apposite that it would be impossible to improve on them. It appears to have had in view three main objects—first, the better and fuller instruction of the people; secondly, the careful and elaborate statement of the case of the Church of England as against the Church of Rome; thirdly, the softening down some of the bitterness produced in the minds of the party of the old learning by the publication of the Ten Articles, and the effecting what was intended to be a happy compromise between the reforming and anti-reforming party. Of this compromise there are abundant traces throughout the whole treatise. Thus Christ's merits are all sufficient for justification, but yet the merits of saints are valuable. Christ is the only mediator and intercessor, but we may ask the saints to pray for us. The Church is both visible and invisible, either a church or a congregation. There are only two orders of ministers in Scripture—priests or bishops, and deacons—but others may be lawfully used. Bishops have a jurisdiction, but a certain liberty is allowable to Christian men. Images are only books for the unlearned, but they may be used and worshipped so long as the honour is given to God. Ceremonies have no power to remit sin, but are very expedient for devotion. Sacraments are seven, but four of them fall short of the other three in dignity.

As 'The Institution of a Christian Man' may be looked upon (as doubtless it was intended to be) as a manifesto of the Church of England as against the Church of Rome, it will be well to quote the words in which it enunciates what may be considered as the foundation principle of the Reformation, viz. the national rights of churches. ' I believe that particular churches, in what place of the world soever they be congregated, be the very parts, portions, or members of the Catholic and Universal Church, and that between them there is indeed no difference in superiority, pre-eminence, or authority, neither that any one of them is head or sovereign over the other; but that they be all equal in power and dignity, and be all grounded and builded upon one foundation. . . . And therefore I do believe that the Church of Rome is not, nor cannot, worthily be called the Catholic Church, but only a particular member thereof, and cannot challenge or vindicate of right and by the Word of God to be head of this Universal Church, or to have any superiority over the other churches of Christ which be in England, France, Spain, or any other realm, but that they be all free from any subjection unto the said Church of Rome, or unto the minister or bishop of the same. . . . And though the said particular churches do much differ one from the other in the divers using and observation of such outward rites, ceremonies, traditions, and ordinances as be instituted by their governors and received and approved among them, yet I believe assuredly that the unity of this Catholic Church cannot therefore, or for that cause, be anything hurted, impeached, or infringed.' The King signed this book hastily, and without having fully considered its contents. There was, in fact, much in it with which he did not agree. The kingly power was not sufficiently magnified, and only a corrective and regulative force was ascribed to the Supremacy. He afterwards had much controversy with Cranmer as to some of its statements, as his notes on his copy, with Cranmer's animadversions on them (still preserved at Oxford), testify. There is evidence that the book was readily welcomed and used by some of the bishops. The Bishop of Exeter directs his clergy to read some part of the explanations of the Paternoster, Ave, Creed, and Commandments, as given in this book, every Sunday to the people. And Bonner, Bishop of London, bids all his clergy procure the book and exercise themselves in the same. Cranmer also published an order that some part of the book should be read every Sunday to the people.

In the year 1537 came out another English version of the Bible, which had been compiled by John Rogers. This contained all of Tyndale's version that he had completed, the gaps being filled from Coverdale's Bible. This version is known as Matthew's Bible, the name of Matthew having been assumed by Rogers. The book was licensed by the King; but it was not considered sufficiently perfect by Cranmer and the bishops, who immediately set on foot a revision of it, which issued in 1539 in the publication of the 'Great Bible.'

Second English Bible

The 'Great Bible'

By an injunction published by the King in 1538, each parish priest is ordered to 'provide one book of the whole Bible of the largest volume in English, and the same set up in some convenient place within your church, whereas your parishioners may most commodiously resort to the same and read it, and that ye discourage no man, privily or apertly, from reading the same Bible, but expressly provoke, stir, and exhort every person to read the same as that which is the very lively Word of God.' The clergy are also bidden to repeat to their parishioners on Sunday, several times over, some portion of the Paternoster, Creed, and Ten Commandments in English. Images which had been abused by pilgrimages or offerings were to be taken down.

The injunction of 1538.

Soon afterwards the tomb of Thomas Becket at Canterbury, which contained an immense accumulation of treasure from the offerings of the faithful for near upon four centuries, was dismantled and rifled by the King's order, and the name of the saint, as an opponent of kings, was ignominiously struck out of the calendar. Twenty-six carts conveyed the treasure to the royal coffers; but the effect of this proceeding was to draw forth from the impetuous Pope, Paul III., the excommunication which had long been held back for politic considerations, and Henry was denounced by Rome as an heretic and apostate from the faith (December 17, 1538).

Rifling of the tomb of St. Thomas

The King excommunicated

In the rapid advancing of the Reformation, Cranmer and Crumwell had no doubt been acting cordially together, while the King was dexterously led by the enormous bribe of the monastic spoils and the riches of St. Thomas to acquiesce in doctrinal statements and an ecclesiastical policy of which he did not really approve. The time now appeared favourable to the heads of the reforming party to make a renewed effort to effect a union between the Church of England and the Lutherans. There can be no doubt that this was the policy of both Cranmer and Crumwell; but the means which they took to bring it about were just such as were most calculated to thwart it. They brought a deputation of Lutheran divines to England[1] (1538), and contrived that they should present their views to the King, censuring those points on which they had as yet been unable to influence

Attempt to procure a union between the Lutherans and the Church of England

---

[1] There was much conference between these divines and Cranmer and the reforming bishops, and an attempt was made to draw up a confession of the reformed faith in Articles. The document which was agreed upon, usually known as the 'Thirteen Articles,' is printed in Cranmer's *Remains*. The substance of it was afterwards embodied in the forty-two articles.

him, viz. communion in one kind, private masses, and the celibacy of the clergy. Henry called Bishop Tonstal to his aid, and immediately proceeded to argue against the Lutheran propositions. The polemical spirit which had led him formerly to write against Luther was roused afresh. He utterly repudiated the Lutherans, and from that moment his whole policy towards the reforming movement was changed. He issued a proclamation proclaiming penalties against married priests. He himself presided at the trial and condemnation of Lambert, or Nicholson, a Sacramentary. Another proclamation ordered the full observance of all the ancient ceremonies. Finally, he replied to the Lutheran objections by procuring the passing of the Six Article Law (1539).

Effects of this attempt on the King

This was the first attempt to make religious doctrine part of the statute law, and to enforce and defend it by terrible penalties. The process is somewhat obscure by which the definition of the doctrines to be thus upheld was arrived at. Six questions, apparently drawn up by the King, were submitted to Convocation and to a committee of the House of Lords, composed of bishops. The reforming party and the anti-reformers were represented on the committee, and no agreement could be arrived at. Then each party was commissioned to draft a Bill, and upon these Bills discussion took place in Parliament. The result was the acceptance by Parliament of the Six Articles in their strongest anti-reforming form. The King had been very busy in procuring this result; but the singular part of the matter is that the Articles ultimately passed were not altogether in accordance with his views. By

The Six Article Law

the first draft of the questions he had shown that he was inclined to accept the Lutheran doctrine of the real presence, without transubstantiation; and by a paper printed among Burnet's 'Records' we find that he was strongly opposed to the necessity of auricular confession. It is probable that, excited by the opposition of the reforming party, and angered by the accounts of the insults offered to religion by the 'Ribauds,' Henry came at last to a more strict view than that with which he had started, and abandoned all thought of compromise. The Act of Parliament after speaking of the need of unity and asserting that the questions had been debated on by the clergy, and that the King had contributed 'high learning and great knowledge' to the discussion, enacts (1) that in the Eucharist there is no longer bread and wine, but the natural body and blood of Christ; (2) that communion in both kinds is not necessary; (3) that priests might not marry; (4) that vows of chastity ought not to be dispensed with; (5) that the use of private masses ought to be continued; (6) that auricular confession was expedient and necessary, and to be retained. Those who spoke, preached, or wrote against the first article were to be burned as heretics, 'without any abjuration.'[1] Those who preached or *obstinately* disputed against the others were to be hanged as felons. Those who in any way spoke against them were to be imprisoned. Married priests were to be separated from their wives; if they returned to them to be hanged as felons, the women to suffer in

[1] The peculiar ferocity of this statute was shown in this refusal of escape by abjuration, which had always been allowed by the ecclesiastical law.

like manner. Those who contemned or abstained from confession or the sacrament of the altar were, for the first offence, to forfeit their goods and be imprisoned; for the second offence to suffer as felons.

It is almost inconceivable that any Parliament should have passed this bloodthirsty law with the in-tention of seriously enforcing it. Accordingly, many writers have endeavoured to show that it was never to any extent enforced. But contemporary records prove that a very considerable number of persons suffered under it. It was, indeed, soon modified, which was not improbably due to the gratitude of the King to Archbishop Cranmer for procuring the sentence of the clergy in their Convocation as to the nullity of his marriage with Anne of Cleves. By this sentence, as by that which decreed the divorce from Anne Boleyn, the too pliant Archbishop and the too obsequious clergy covered themselves with disgrace.

Obsequiousness of Cranmer and the clergy

The triumph of the anti-reforming party led to the attainder and death of Crumwell. The King had obtained by his means all the spoil he was likely to secure from the Church, and now threw aside his instrument, with whom, for other causes, he was dissatisfied.

Fall of Crumwell, 1540

The anti-reformers had gained much, but they by no means felt secure. Cranmer was known to be in high favour with the King, and might at any time launch him again on the path of reform. 'The Institution of a Christian Man' was still the authorised exposition of doctrine, which in the view of many was heretical and mischievous. Cranmer therefore, at all hazards, must be destroyed, and the

Policy of the anti-reforming party

'Institution' superseded. The attempt to bring about the first of these objects failed, Cranmer being too useful to the King to be abandoned. The attempt to overthrow the 'Institution' and to check the reading of the English Bible was to a certain extent successful. A curious anticipatory Act of Parliament was passed (July 1540) called an Act concerning the 'constitution and declaration of the Christian religion,' which enacted that whatsoever should be determined by a committee of divines appointed for that purpose, and approved by the King, should be received and believed by all the King's subjects, but that nothing should be sanctioned by this Act contrary to the laws and statutes of the realm.

An attempt was made by the committee of divines to draw up a document without the knowledge of Cranmer, and, having obtained the King's license, suddenly to spring it upon the Archbishop—who, it was thought, seeing the royal signature, would be compelled to accept it. This, however, failed. Cranmer, who was not so pliant in his theology as in his administration, refused to sign. The Archbishop then issued a series of questions to some leading divines on points which were to be treated of in the new book. The answers which remain (in Burnet and Strype) show a strange confusion in the minds of the writers between the secular and the ecclesiastical. It would seem as if the overbearing dogmatism of the King had thrown the minds of the divines quite off their balance, and everything is interpreted with reference to his claims of autocracy. The King has, according to some of the answers, the 'cure of souls'

Formation of 'The Erudition of any Christian Man'

of all his people; he can make bishops and priests—all ecclesiastical jurisdiction is from him. The outcome, however, of these preparations was, on the whole, satisfactory. The book now constructed—called 'The Erudition of any Christian Man'—follows generally the lines of the 'Institution,' though the language is different. It begins with an article on faith, which the first book had not. On the sacrament of the altar the 'Institution' had taught that the natural body and blood of Christ is 'contained and comprehended' under the form of bread and wine. The 'Erudition' teaches that the bread and wine is 'changed and turned to the very substance of the body and blood.' There is added a long exhortation as to the preparation for receiving. The 'Erudition' speaks of 'bishops *and* priests,' not 'bishops *or* priests,' and declares the 'succession from the Apostles.' It has a stronger declaration of the King's ecclesiastical supremacy than the first book. This very useful book, having been first accepted by Convocation, was published in May, 1543, and was generally known as the 'King's Book,' as distinguished from the 'Institution,' called the 'Bishops' Book.' The anti-reforming party had thus found that the chief thing which they had to dread was the continued influence of Archbishop Cranmer with the King. This had availed to bring about a modification of the Six Article Law; to prevent the suppression of the English Bible under the pretence of a new revision by the bishops (1542); to make the attempt to overthrow the 'Institution' issue in the publication of the 'Erudition'; and it also availed to bring out, under the King's sanction, the Litany in English

(1544), and in 1545 to produce what was known as the 'King's Primer,' a book of English prayers and religious pieces, which schoolmasters were to teach to the young, and which all were invited to use. The preface of this book strongly stated the importance of all religious services being in the vulgar tongue, that 'all may know both what they pray, and also with what words.'

The 'King's Primer'

These publications were coincident with a work of great importance, which, under the sanction and direction of the Archbishop, was being carried on in the Convocation of Canterbury. On February 24, 1542, Cranmer introduced the question of the examination and correction of the old service-books. As such work could only be done by a committee, it is probable that a committee was at this time appointed. In the following February the Archbishop informed the House that the King desired that all the service-books should be thoroughly corrected, and 'castigated from all manner of mention of the Bishop of Rome's name; from all apocryphas, feigned legends, superstitious orations, collects, versicles and responses, and that the services should be made out of Scripture or other authentic doctors.' This was the foundation of the English Prayer-book. The only results of the labours of this committee, published during this reign, were the English Litany, an English version of the Lord's Prayer, the Ten Commandments, and the 'Hail, Mary.' These, together with a chapter of the Old Testament and a chapter of the New Testament from the English Bible, were to be read in all churches every Sunday. As early as 1542 Cranmer

The Liturgical Revision

Archbishop Cranmer's work

also introduced in Convocation the subject of preparing a book of English Homilies.

Thus the Archbishop, whose subservience to the King in the scandalous proceedings of his divorce cases has brought upon his memory deserved reproach, was, in the matter of the religious reformation, of the highest value to the Church of England. There was apparently no other divine in a place of influence who cared much for the furtherance of this work, while there were many who were bitterly hostile to it. Occasionally their influence predominated, as in the proclamations of 1543 and 1546, restricting the reading of the Bible. But, upon the whole, the reforming process went steadily forward under Cranmer's guidance, and he retained his exceptional favour with the King to the last. At this period probably his sentiments were more Lutheran than anything else ; but he was in a transition state, and in the next reign he adopted views on the Eucharist different from those which he now held.

The chief opponent of Cranmer's religious policy was Gardiner, Bishop of Winchester, who also had first risen through the divorce case, who had zealously defended the ecclesiastical supremacy, and been content to take the royal license for the exercise of his episcopal jurisdiction. Gardiner was an able man; more of a canonist than a divine ; not very honest apparently, and hence not so fully trusted by the King as Cranmer, as his omission from the Council appointed by the King's will proved. But Cranmer's work might never have been carried out, there might have been no English Bible, no Ten Articles or 'Institution,' no reforming Primers, nor Proclamations

Bishop Gardiner

against Ceremonies, had it not been for the tact, boldness, and skill of Thomas Crumwell, who influenced the King more directly and constantly than Cranmer, and who knew how to make his influence acceptable by an unprincipled confiscation and an absurd exaggeration of the royal supremacy. Crumwell knew that in his master's heart there was a dislike and contempt of the clergy, and a scorn of all clerical claims, when he induced him to issue in 1535 his appointment as Vicar-General, couched in terms studiously offensive to the clergy, and sweeping away at a blow all the liberties of the Church; and when, as a sequel to this, he led him to declare the suspension of the jurisdiction of all bishops, who were to be restored to it only on taking out licenses from the Crown. It is probable that Crumwell's policy was simply irreligious, and only directed towards preserving his influence with the King; but as the support of the reforming part of the nation was a useful factor in it, he was thus led to push forward religious reformation in conjunction with Cranmer.

Thomas Crumwell

It has been before said that purity and disinterestedness are not to be looked for in all the actors in the English Reformation. To this it may be added that neither in the movement itself nor in those who took part in it is to be found complete consistency. This, indeed, is not to be wondered at. Men were feeling their way along untrodden paths, without any very clear perception of the end at which they were aiming, or any perfect understanding of the situation. The King had altogether misapprehended the meaning of his supremacy. A host

Character of the religious history of the period

of divines, whose views as to the distinction between the secular and the spiritual had been confused by the action of the Popes, helped to mislead him. The clergy, accustomed to be crushed and humiliated by the Popes, submitted to be crushed and humiliated by the King; and as the tide of his autocratic temper ebbed and flowed, yielded to each change. Hence there was action and reaction throughout the reign. But in this there were obvious advantages for the Church. The gradual process accustomed men's thoughts to a reformation which should not be drastic or iconoclastic, but rather conservative and deliberate. In this temper men came to meet the sudden laxity and commotions of the next reign, when there was especial need for a thoughtful and judicious deliberateness to check the haste and hurry of the more violent reformers.

CHAPTER VI.

THE UNSETTLING CAUSED BY THE ACCESSION OF EDWARD VI.

1547–1549.

IN the Council which was appointed by King Henry's will to be the administrators of affairs under the boy King Edward, views favourable to sweeping alterations in religion quickly gained the ascendent. Bishop Gardiner was not a member of the Council, Bishop Tonstal was soon got rid of, and the direction of affairs fell into the hands of the Lord Protector, the Earl of Hertford, and Archbishop Cranmer. Cranmer, though his views were not opposed to Erastianism, happily had the element of caution and moderation. He had taken an active part and lively interest in the labours of Convocation during the latter years of Henry's reign, and it might fairly be hoped that he would not now depreciate or neglect the result of its deliberations. The Lord Protector was without genuine care for the Church or for religion, and was chiefly intent on strengthening his position, and obtaining spoils from ecclesiastical property. The first measures of the reign were ominous. 'The young King and his ministers,' writes Bishop Stubbs, 'entertained ideas which, if they had been fully developed, must have ended in the destruction of the older ecclesiastical system.'

Policy of King Edward's Council

But now came in the salutary check furnished by the action of Convocation, and by the work in which it had been employed during the latter years of Henry's reign. The Convocation addressed the Archbishop, who had shown himself inclined to act rather as a Minister of State than as Primate, demanding its proper share in the work concerning the Church which was in progress. There was an evident intention to put the clergy aside altogether; but they returned to the charge, and finally succeeded so far that though there were irregularities enough, there was nevertheless no change made in the Church services and religious standards in this reign quite independently of the recognised clerical body. Throughout the reign we see two opposing forces at work—the eager reforming movement represented by Hooper, the calm, constructive spirit, represented by the First Prayer-book.

The check of Convocation

The first act affecting the Church determined upon by the Council of the young King was the holding of a general royal visitation, such as had been designed in 1535, when Crumwell was made Vicar-General, but which had then been confined to the monasteries. With a view to this visitation all episcopal jurisdiction was suspended. The King's letter to the Archbishop of York informs him 'that inasmuch we, by our supreme royal authority, have determined to visit all and singular ecclesiastical places, and the clergy and the people,' therefore the Archbishop is strictly forbidden, either by himself or his deputies, to exercise any jurisdiction; only he is commanded to inhibit all bishops and priests from preaching anywhere save where they were legally entitled to preach. Great preparations were made for this visitation. There were to be civilians, divines, and secretaries, as well as

The first royal visitation

persons described simply as 'gentlemen.' England was divided into six districts for the purposes of the visitation.

The visitors were to take with them a book of Homilies, some of which were probably drawn up in the last reign, as there was an order of Convocation that this should be done, and some were now added, composed by Cranmer. These Homilies were plain sermons on the chief doctrines of Christianity and on Christian practice. They were divided into parts, not in their length overtaxing the patience of the hearers. There was not much controversial matter in them, but in the third part of the sermon on good works there is a lively attack on the old superstitions which it was desired to eradicate. As there were then but few priests in England competent to preach in English, and fewer still inclined to preach such doctrine as was desired by the authorities, these Homilies were designed to take the place of sermons when the parish priest was either unable to preach, or was inhibited from preaching his own words. In a short time, when all preaching was forbidden; the Homilies became the only instruction allowed to the people, and doubtless they had a great effect in advancing the Reformation movement.

The Homilies

Another chief work of the visitors was to leave with each church a body of 'Injunctions,' which may be regarded as a formal attempt to construct the Reformation settlement. These Injunctions had the force of an Act of Parliament, and could not lightly be disregarded. They professed to be drawn up for ' the advancement of the true honour of Almighty

The first Injunctions of Edward VI.

God, the suppression of idolatry and superstition throughout the King's realms and dominions, and for planting true religion, to the extirpation of all hypocrisy, enormities and abuses.' The first enjoins all persons having the cure of souls four times a year to declare the abolishing of the Bishop of Rome's 'usurped power and jurisdiction,' and to set forth the King's supremacy. Once a quarter also such persons shall 'make or cause to be made' a sermon 'purely and sincerely declaring the Word of God,' and condemning the old superstitious image-worship as idolatry. Then all images which have been 'abused with pilgrimage and offering' are ordered to be removed.[1] On holy days when there is no sermon, the priest is to recite from the pulpit the Paternoster, Credo, and Ten Commandments in English. He is charged to see that the Sacraments be duly administered, and that within three months 'one book of the whole Bible, of the largest volume in English,' be procured,[2] and within twelve months the 'Paraphrases of Erasmus, also in English, upon the Gospels,' which are to be set up in some convenient place in the churches, to which the parishioners can have free access. The parishioners are to be examined in Lent whether they can say the Creed, the Paternoster, and the Ten Commandments in English, as a necessary preliminary to the reception of the Holy Communion. Parish registers are to be carefully kept, and all beneficed clergy are to distribute a certain proportion of their

[1] These Injunctions embodied and repeated those of 1538, but with large additions.
[2] Bibles probably were already to be found in most churches, having been prescribed by the Injunctions of 1538.

income to the poor, and be liable to repair the chancels of their churches and their 'mansions' up to the fifth part of their benefice. At high mass the Epistle and Gospel are to be read in English, and at matins one chapter of the New Testament immediately after the lections, and at evensong after Magnificat one chapter of the Old Testament. Processions are to be disused, and the Litany in English is to be said 'in the midst of the church.' The Lord's day is to be strictly observed, but in the time of harvest men might labour on that day. All vain ceremonies are to be abandoned, and all 'pictures, paintings, and monuments of feigned miracles, pilgrimages, idolatry, and superstition to be destroyed,' whether on walls, glass windows, or otherwise, and a pulpit set up in every church. One of the Homilies is to be read every Sunday, at which time 'the prime and hours' are to be omitted. A new form of the 'Bidding Prayer' is given.[1] In this, prayer for the dead is enjoined, but only in general terms. Special injunctions were given to the bishops to see that these directions were obeyed. They are also charged to preach within their dioceses at least four times a year, and to be very careful in giving Orders. The Injunctions seem to have been generally received without much opposition, but Bishops Gardiner and Bonner made strong protests against them, and were committed to the Fleet prison.

Gardiner and Bonner committed to prison

Parliament met on November 4. Its first act was of a religious character, and a necessary supplement to

---

[1] The old form of 'bidding of bedes,' which is very lengthy, is printed by Burnet in the Records from *The Festival* (Edw. VI. No. viii.).

the injunctions. It ordained that from henceforth Holy Communion should be given to the laity in both kinds. This act was founded upon a resolution of the Convocation of Canterbury, passed November 30, and received the royal assent on December 20, 1547. It recited the great reverence due to that Holy Sacrament, and ordered that it should be offered to all in both kinds. It is probable that the service for this was already prepared. It is known that it was the wish of King Henry to have an English mass, and the Convocation Committee—which since 1543 had been employed on the recasting of the services —had probably arrived at an agreement as to the service which now appeared. According to Heylin a committee of divines was appointed to review and approve this service. This committee he conjectures to have consisted of the same persons who shortly afterwards were engaged in the construction of the First Book of Common Prayer, viz. Cranmer, Archbishop of Canterbury; Goodrich, Bishop of Ely; Holbech, Bishop of Lincoln; Day, Bishop of Chichester; Skyp, Bishop of Hereford; Thirlby, Bishop of Westminster; Ridley, Bishop of Rochester; Cox, Dean of Christ Church; May, Dean of St. Paul's; Taylor, Dean of Lincoln; Heynes, Dean of Exeter; Robertson, afterwards Dean of Durham; Redmayne, Master of Trinity, Cambridge. 'Taking into consideration,' says Heylin, ' as well the right use of Scripture as the usage of the Primitive Church, they agreed to such a form and order as might comply with the intention of the King and the Act of Parliament, without giving any just offence to the Romish party.' The plan which they adopted was to

First English Communion Office

leave the Latin mass unaltered up to the end of the canon and the communion of the priest, and to add to it in English a form of communion for the people. The English part of this office was with some small variations reproduced in the Prayer-book of 1549, and has survived, very justly, all the various reviews to which the Prayer-book has been subjected. It was published March, 1548, by a proclamation, in which men were exhorted to 'receive it with such obedience and conformity that the King might be encouraged from time to time further to travail for the Reformation, and setting forth of such godly orders as may be most to God's glory, the edifying of our subjects, and the advancement of true religion; which thing we, by the help of God, most earnestly intend to bring to good effect, wishing all our loving subjects in the meantime to stay and quiet themselves with our direction, as men content to follow authority, and not enterprising to run afore, and so by their rashness become the greatest hinderers of such things as they more arrogantly than godly would seem most hotly to put forward.'

The proclamation for the new Communion Office

The calm wisdom of these words contrasted somewhat strangely with some of the acts of those in authority. Bishop Ridley had, as it seems without any legal justification, begun to cause the demolition of altars in his diocese of Rochester. By an Act of Parliament bishops were to be appointed simply by letters patent; they were not only obliged to take out commissions for the exercise of their office, but held their sees during good behaviour, and exercised their jurisdiction only under the King, their writs

Violent legislation

running in his name and their seals bearing the royal arms. By another Act all chantries, hospitals, and colleges were granted anew to the Crown. These Acts exhibit the spirit then too prevalent, of the determination to force the new state of things on an unconvinced and uninstructed people.

Throughout the year 1548 one proclamation succeeds another, bearing witness to the troubled state of things.

<small>Proclamations of the year 1548</small> By one the people are forbidden to 'innovate' or leave undone any ceremonies which were legal in the last reign. By another, the absolute removal of all images from churches is ordered. Another enjoins upon preachers prudence and forbearance; but as this proved ineffective, another proclamation inhibited preaching altogether. Irreverence was terribly on the increase. Proclamations forbade quarrelling and shouting in churches, bringing horses and mules into churches, mobbing and ill-treating of priests, stealing sacred vessels and church furniture. The old system of religious worship stood condemned, and as yet there was no new system perfected to take its place.

One curious effect of the disjointed state of things which prevailed in the year 1548 was the formation <small>Unauthorised services</small> and use of private and unauthorised English services. The preamble to the first Act of Uniformity speaks of 'divers and sundry forms and fashions' of Matins and Evensong and of the Communion office, and 'divers and sundry rites and ceremonies concerning the same.' Indeed, some of these service books have been discovered. They were due to the impatience of men at the calm and cautious

F 2

action of the body of divines at Windsor, who were carefully compiling the First English Prayer-book.

The delay was certainly not more than the importance of the task confided to the body of divines absolutely required; but at this critical moment it was unfortunate, as giving occasion to the outbreak of the wildest fantasies. 'Alas!' writes Hooper, 'not only are those heresies reviving among us which were formerly dead and buried, but new ones are springing up every day. There are such libertines and wretches as are daring enough in their conventicles not only to deny that Christ is the Messiah and Saviour of the world, but also to call that blessed seed a mischievous fellow, and a deceiver of the world. On the other hand a great portion of the kingdom so adheres to the Popish faction as altogether to set at nought God and the lawful authority of the magistrates.' It must have been, therefore, with the most lively satisfaction that many heard that the divines at Windsor had at last finished their task, and that the new service book had been brought into Convocation some time in November, 1548.

Wild opinions

CHAPTER VII.

THE FIRST ENGLISH PRAYER-BOOK.

1549-50.

As soon as Archbishop Cranmer was set free by the death of Henry VIII. from the difficulties which stood in the way of co-operation with the German divines, he proceeded at once to carry out his long-cherished scheme of close intercourse with the leading men among them. He had for fifteen years been married to a German lady, the niece of Osiander, the pastor of Nuremberg. His acquaintance with the chief Lutherans was considerable, and though as yet he looked with somewhat of suspicion on the Genevan and French school of reformers, he still was willing to take them into counsel—his favourite project being to promulgate a confession, or declaration of doctrine, by all the chief reformers, in opposition to the decrees of the Council of Trent. In July 1548 Cranmer writes to the Pole, John a Lasco, that they had invited all the learned men, and scarcely had to lament the absence of any of them, save himself and Melanchthon. A Lasco soon afterwards came to England; but neither Melanchthon on the one hand, nor Calvin nor Bullinger on the other, responded to the invitation. Among the earliest arrivals were Peter Martyr, a Florentine by birth, and Martin Bucer, an Alsatian. They were both learned men, and were settled by the Archbishop in the divinity professorships of Oxford and Cambridge. Neither of

Cranmer's invitations to foreign reformers

them could be said to symbolise altogether either with Luther or Calvin. They inclined, however, more towards the latter than the former, especially on the subject of the Eucharist, and their views soon produced a marked effect upon those of the Archbishop.

No trace of this, however, is to be found in the First English Prayer-book, although Cranmer's previous connection with Lutheranism, and especially with Nuremberg, had exercised considerable influence upon the services which had now been prepared for the use of the English Church. In the first Communion office the Consultation of Archbishop Herman of Cologne, adapted by Bucer and Melanchthon from the Nuremberg office, had furnished the subject matter of the exhortation, the confession, and the comfortable words, which were reproduced in the book of 1549. Other parts of the English book, as the Litany and the Baptismal services, owed something to the Consultation. But with this exception the Prayer-book now compiled for the use of the English Church owed nothing to the foreign reformers. Calvin had signified his views about what was fitting for such a book in a letter to the Protector in the autumn of 1548; but there is no trace of his opinions having had any influence on the compilers. Bucer and Martyr criticised the book when it appeared, and found many faults in it. It is clear they had no hand in framing it.

Amount of influence of foreign reformers on the English Prayer-book

The book was, in fact, substantially, and almost entirely, an adaptation of the ancient Breviary and sacramental offices of the Sarum Custom Book, and in its character illustrated the triumph of the moderate and Catholic party over the more violent and drastic reformers. The Morning Prayer is formed from the ancient offices of matins, laud, and prime; the Evening Prayer from those of vespers and compline. The intermediate hours of tierce and sext do not contribute much to the English office. As a matter of fact, though the services for Seven Hours are given in the Breviary, these were not ordinarily said separately, except in the monasteries, but by an aggregation similar to that which was carried out in the English book, were made into two services, between which mass was said. The English book therefore followed the ancient usage in this respect, and with regard to 'the Supper of the Lord, and the Holy Communion, commonly called the Mass,' it followed the Sarum missal in all essentials, providing carefully for the sacrificial character of the service, directing the mixing of water with the wine, and the use of the ancient vestments.

The book mainly an adaptation of the ancient offices

Such a book coming forth by authority in those troublous and excited times may well be regarded as a special and peculiar gift to the Church, and it is hardly too much to say of it that it was the salvation of the Church of England. The book appears to have been laid before the Convocation of Canterbury in November or early in December. In the absence of the Convocation Records this has sometimes been doubted; but one fact sufficiently proves it, viz. that in a letter to Bishop Bonner, who scrupled about the use of the book, the Council allege that 'the book was approved and set forth by the bishops and all other learned men of the realm in their synods

Great value of the book

Approved by Convocation

and convocations provincial.' This could not have been alleged to Bishop Bonner, who must have been perfectly cognisant of the facts, had he been able to disprove it.

The Act of Uniformity establishing the book was read a first time in the House of Commons on December 19, and in the Lords on the following day. The introduction of the Prayer-book had been preceded by a public disputation on the Eucharist, in which almost all the bishops took part. This is said to have been held in the Parliament House, but probably was not part of the regular proceedings of Parliament, but an extraordinary arrangement to facilitate the passing of the Act of Uniformity. As it was, there was a very strong opposition made to the Act in the House of Lords by the bishops of the 'old learning,' three even of those who had been appointed to compile the book—Day, Skyp, and Thirlby—protesting against it. Finally the Act passed the Lords January 15, and the Commons January 21, 1549, thus falling within the second year of King Edward. The general use of the new service-book was prescribed to commence on Whit Sunday, June 9, and heavy penalties were enacted for those who should refuse to use it, or should 'deprave it.'[1]

Established by law

The grounds upon which the acceptance of the new book was based in the preface were: first, the more full

---

[1] The first edition was published at the beginning of March. An order as to the price was inserted, which varies somewhat in the various editions. In one copy the book unbound is to be sold for 2s. 2d, in another 2s. 6d, and 'bound in paste or in boards not above the price of 4s. the piece.'

The First English Prayer-book 73

and orderly reading of Holy Scripture, very little of which found a place in the old services; secondly, the omission of 'vain and superstitious' matters;

The preface

thirdly, the use of the English language, enabling the people to understand the services in which they were taking a part; fourthly, the introduction of uniformity, thereby getting rid of the great variety in the services previously existing from the prevalence of various 'uses' in different parts of the kingdom.

The book being essentially of a moderate type was not of a nature calculated to please the extreme men on either side. The violent reformers were extremely angry and indignant. Hooper, afterwards a bishop, thus writes to Bullinger: 'I can scarcely express to you,

Unpleasing to the more violent Reformers

my dear friend, under what difficulties and dangers we are labouring and struggling that the idol of the Mass may be thrown out. It is no small hindrance to our exertions that the form which our Senate or Parliament, as we commonly call it, has prescribed for the whole realm, is so very defective and of doubtful construction, and in some respects indeed manifestly impious. I am so much offended with that book, and that not without abundant reason, that, if it be not corrected, I neither can nor will communicate with the Church in the administration of the Lord's Supper.'

On the other hand, partly from dislike of the changes in religious worship, but more, probably, from

To the common people

anger at the enclosure of the commons and social grievances, the people rose in Sussex, Hampshire, Kent, Gloucestershire, Suffolk, Warwickshire, Essex, Hertfordshire, Leicestershire, Worcestershire, and Rutlandshire. These risings were easily put down, but one in Devonshire was more difficult to deal with. These insurgents sent up a paper of formal demands for the restoration of all the old superstitions. They desired that the Bible should be suppressed, 'since otherwise the clergy could not easily confound the heretics,' and that 'the new service should be laid aside, since it was like a Christmas game.' Archbishop Cranmer replied to this paper, answering all their objections. To their censure of the new service book he said, 'The old service had many ludicrous things in it. The new was simple and grave; if it appeared ridiculous to them, it was as the gospel was long ago, foolishness to the Greeks.' This very serious outbreak, as well as that in Norfolk under Ket, was not put down without great difficulty and much bloodshed. It may be assumed from these general commotions throughout England that the new service book was by no means popular with the common people, who were naturally much under the influence of the priests.

These men, very few of whom cared for reformation, had all their lives been accustomed to say the Latin services in a conventional way, and when the English service was forced upon them, they tried to impress the same sort of character upon this. They had their frequent Masses, now called Communions; and their bowing and kissing, their gestures and tones, were those of the old ceremonial. The services, though now put into the English language, might still be used in such a way that they would not be 'understanded of the people.' In July 1549 the Council wrote to Bishop Bonner that 'the book so much travailed for, and also sincerely set forth,

Attempts to give the book the character of the old services

THE FIRST ENGLISH PRAYER-BOOK 75

remaineth in many places of this our realm either not known at all, or not used, or at the least if it be used, very seldom, and that in such light and irreverent sort as the people in many places have heard nothing; or if they hear, they neither understand, nor have that spiritual delectation in the same, that to good Christians appertaineth.' Evidently the mere publication of the book was not sufficient. Some further measures must be taken to insure its proper use.

With this view a second Royal Visitation took place in the summer of 1549. Among the articles or inquisitions left by the Visitors we find, 'That no minister do counterfeit the Popish Mass, as to kiss the Lord's Table; washing his fingers at every time of the Communion; blessing his eyes with the paten or sudary; or crossing his head with the paten; shifting of the book from one place to the other; laying down and licking the chalice of the Communion; holding up his fingers, hands, or thumbs joined toward his temples; breathing upon the bread or chalice; showing the Sacrament openly before the distribution of the Communion; ringing or sacring bells; or setting any light upon the Lord's board at any time; and finally to use no other ceremonies than are appointed in the King's Book of Common-prayers, or kneeling otherwise than is in the said book.'

Second Royal Visitation

The great upholder of this plan for giving a character to the English book which it was not intended to bear, was Bonner, Bishop of London, and, in consequence, after some attempts had been made without success to cause him to change his policy, he was brought before a mixed commission.

Bishop Bonner deprived

The principal charge against him was that he had not asserted, as he had been required to do, that the King's nonage did not interfere with his sovereign authority; but the fact that he was the leading antagonist of the Reformation was doubtless chiefly in the minds of the commissioners. He was deprived of his bishopric (October 1549) and committed to the Tower.

The service-book, in consideration of the distracted and unsettled state of things, had been published with all possible speed, and without waiting for the construction of an Ordinal which should be in accordance with the rest of the book. The task of making this was now committed to six prelates, and 'six other men learned in God's law' (whether divines or not does not appear). An Act of Parliament gave legal force to the Ordinal when it should be made and ratified, and on February 28, 1550, it was laid before the Council. Eleven of the commissioners signed it, Heath, Bishop of Worcester, alone refusing. For this he was very unjustly, as it seems, committed to the Fleet prison. The character of this Ordinal was the same with that of the Prayer-book, to which it was designed to be annexed. It retained somewhat of the old ceremonial in combination with newly-introduced prayers and passages of Scripture. It differed in some respects from the Ordinal which immediately succeeded it, but in substance the two were identical. In the first Ordinal the persons to be ordained were to be vested in white albs plain. The deacon who was to read the Gospel was to put on a tunicle. The ordination of a priest was accompanied by the giving the chalice and paten. The bishop to be consecrated, as

The first reformed Ordinal

THE FIRST ENGLISH PRAYER-BOOK 77

well as the consecrators, was to wear a surplice with a cope. The Bible was to be laid upon his neck with an exhortation. The pastoral staff to be placed in his hands with another exhortation. These things were afterwards omitted in the revised Ordinal, whether wisely or not may be doubted.

In order to assist the establishment of the new book, and to overthrow the hopes of those who were building on the disgrace of the Duke of Somerset an expectation of the reversal of the Reformation, an order was issued to Archbishop Cranmer by the Council (February 1550), which recited 'That divers unquiet and evil-disposed persons, since the apprehension of the Duke of Somerset, have noised and bruited abroad that they should have again their old Latin service, their conjured bread and water, with suchlike vain and superstitious ceremonies, as though the setting forth of that book had been the only act of the said duke; We, therefore, by the advice of the body and state of our Privy Council, not only considering the said book to be our act and the act of the whole state of our realm assembled together in Parliament, but also the same to be grounded upon Holy Scripture . . . to put away all such vain expectation of having the public service again in the Latin tongue, do require and charge you that you do command the dean and prebendaries of the cathedral church, the parson, vicar, or curate and churchwardens of every parish within your diocere, to bring and deliver unto you or your deputy all Antiphoners, Missals, Grails, Processionals, Manuals, Legends, Pies, Portasies, Journals, and Ordinals after the use of Sarum, Lincoln,

Order to destroy the old service-books

York, or any other private use, and all other books of service the keeping whereof should be a let to the usage of the Book of Common-prayers, and that you take the same books into your hands and them so deface and abolish that they never hereafter serve to any such use as they were provided for.' This violent order [1] against the old service-books, which might at least have been removed with reverence, was the commencement of a more thoroughgoing and drastic policy in Church matters.

Of a piece with it was the attack now made upon the ancient altars of the Church. The credit, or otherwise, of originating this must be given to Bishop Ridley. He had commenced to attack the altars, without legal right, as it seems, in the diocese of Rochester, and when translated to London he continued the same policy. In his 'Injunctions,' published in the summer of 1550, it is said, 'Whereas in divers places some use the Lord's board after the form of a table, and some as an altar, whereby dissension is perceived to arise among the unlearned; therefore, wishing a godly unity to be observed in all our diocese, and for that the form of a table may move more and turn the simple from the old superstitious opinions of the Popish Mass, and to the right use of the Lord's Supper, we exhort the curates, churchwardens, and questmen here present to erect and set up the Lord's board after the form of an honest table decently covered . . . and to take down and abolish all other by-altars or tables.' This policy strongly commending itself to the Council, an order was issued to Bishop Ridley and

Altars ordered to be removed

---

[1] This order was afterwards repeated in an Act of Parliament.

the other bishops (November 1550) to cause all the altars in every church and chapel to be taken down, and instead of them 'a table to be set up in some convenient part of the chancel.' One bishop at least, Day of Chichester, refused to obey this order, it being, as he said, against his conscience to do so. In the tyrann'cal spirit which now prevailed, Bishop Day was committed to prison. Day had been selected as one of the compilers of the Prayer-book, but had not been able to accept it in its completed form. Together with Skyp, Bishop of Hereford, and Thirlby, of Westminster, he had opposed in the House of Lords the legalising of the Book. This opposition may have had something to do with the harshness with which he was treated. Everything now pointed towards a complete and entire transformation of the religious status of the country. The young King's new advisers were still more reckless and unscrupulous than the last. The more the thoroughness and simplicity of the Geneva Reformation could be furthered, the more Church plunder would fall into the hands of the courtiers. From this point a strong and decided movement in the 'Protestant' direction sets in.

CHAPTER VIII.

THE DOCTRINAL CONFESSION AND THE MANUALS OF THIS REIGN.

1547–1553.

THE exhibition of the reforming spirit in matters of doctrine in this reign must be sought for not so much in the Prayer-book as in the Doctrinal Confession and the Manuals of Instruction. In these the Archbishop led the way in his 'Homilies on Salvation, on Faith, and on Good Works.' It is probable also that he had a principal share in the composition of the other homilies. His style is homely, but very plain and instructive, and well suited for teaching uneducated people.

Cranmer's homilies

In 1548 Archbishop Cranmer put out a catechism translated into English from a Latin translation of the German original made by Justus Jonas. This catechism consists of a series of sermons on the Articles of the Creed, the Lord's Prayer, the Ten Commandments, and the Sacraments. Coming as it did from a Lutheran source, we are not surprised to find in it strong assertions of the corporal presence in the Eucharist, though the Archbishop subsequently maintained that there was nothing in it which might not be interpreted spiritually. It is not probable that this catechism had much to do with the spread of the Reformation. It is heavy and dull in style and not likely to be attractive to young people. Its translator and publisher soon passed to another terminology and dif-

The Lutheran catechism

ferent statements on the Eucharist, and a little afterwards sanctioned another catechism of which more will be said hereafter.

It was some time about the year 1548 that Archbishop Cranmer abandoned the doctrine of the Lutherans on the Eucharist, and accepted that medium position between Lutheranism and Zwinglianism which was advocated by Martyr and Bucer. He himself ascribes this change in his views to the influence of Dr. Ridley, formerly his chaplain, and always his constant friend. He now decided to give expression to his opinions in a book called 'A Defence of the true and catholic doctrine of the Sacrament of the Body and Blood of our Saviour Christ.' This book greatly pleased the Zwinglians. John a Lasco writes to Bullinger, 'The Archbishop of Canterbury, a man of singular worth and learning, has, contrary to the general expectation, delivered his opinion upon this subject learnedly, correctly, orderly, and clearly.' The uncompromising Hooper was not, however, altogether satisfied. He writes, 'The Archbishop of Canterbury has relaxed much of his Lutheranism (whether all of it I cannot say). He is not so decided as I could wish, and dares not, I fear, assert his opinion in all respects.' The book commences with a very solemn preface, and is written in that simple and plain style of which the Archbishop was a singular master. He declares that he proposes to treat the subject 'so sincerely and plainly, without doubts, ambiguities, or vain questions, that the very simple and unlearned people may easily understand the same and be edified thereby.' It may therefore be regarded more as a manual of instruction for the people

Cranmer's 'Treatise on the Eucharist'

than as a controversial treatise, though it immediately involved its author in controversy with Bishop Gardiner and Dr. Smith.

From the very beginning of the reign, in the midst of his manifold employments, Cranmer had never lost sight of that which was nearest his heart, namely, the setting forth by authority a confession of faith, which should state the doctrines of the reformed churches as against the canons then being fashioned at Trent. It was for this purpose that he invited, one after another, the leading advocates of the Reformation from abroad, desiring, as he writes to Bullinger, 'That in England or elsewhere there might be convoked a synod of the most learned and excellent persons, in which provision might be made for the purity of ecclesiastical doctrine, and especially for an agreement upon the Sacramentarian controversy.' Cranmer had not forgotten how, twenty years before, he had conferred with the Lutheran divines then in England and had arrived at a substantial agreement on thirteen articles based on the Confession of Augsburg, which only failed of being enacted from Henry's jealousy of foreign interference. These articles he proposed now to promulgate and ratify, and to combine with them others which should cover all the main points on which difference of opinion might arise. An Order in Council in the beginning of 1551 directed the Archbishop to proceed in this work. The method adopted appears to have been for Cranmer and Ridley to make drafts of the articles and forward these to such bishops and divines as it was thought could be trusted, for their animadversions. Some of the foreign divines in England were

[margin: Formation of the 42 Articles]

no doubt applied to for their criticisms, but there is no
distinct record of this being done. Two of the most
prominent of them, Bucer and Paul Fagius, were now
dead, and there was none perhaps with whom Cranmer
altogether symbolised, except Peter Martyr. John
a Lasco was, however, a bosom friend of the Archbishop,
and it is not improbable that some of the suggestions of
this talented Zwinglian may have found a place in the
Articles. In May 1552 the Council desired that the
draft of the Confession might be laid before them.
This was done, and it was returned to the Archbishop
for some emendations. He then presented it to the
King. The King gave it for review to his six chaplains,
who sent it again to the Archbishop, accompanied by
some suggestions, and with a request that it should be
returned at once to his Majesty. The very next day
Cranmer returned it. There was evidently great eagerness on the part of Edward to get the matter finished.
From this fact a strong presumption arises that the
Articles when finished were laid before the Convocation.
For, in spite of the eagerness with which they had been
pressed forward to completion, they were not published
till May in the following year, when the clergy were
invited to subscribe them. Convocation had met in
March 1553, and it is almost certain must then have
received and sanctioned the Articles, its assent having
been waited for before their promulgation. The title of
the Articles asserts that they were agreed upon in the
Synod of London in 1552 (N.S. 1553) and this assertion
is repeated in the title of the catechism presently to be
mentioned. There is therefore no good reason for
doubting this fact, especially as ten years afterwards, in

the Convocation held under Queen Elizabeth, the assertion was emphatically repeated.[1] Now if the Convocation gave a formal sanction to the Forty-two Articles in March 1553, it also thereby gave a formal sanction to the Second Prayer-book, by the Thirty-fifth Article, which declares, 'The book which of very late time was given to the Church of England by the King's authority and the Parliament, containing the manner and form of praying and ministering the Sacraments in the Church of England; likewise also the book of ordering ministers of the Church set forth by the aforesaid authority, are godly, and in no point repugnant to the wholesome doctrine of the Gospel, but agreeable thereto, furthering and beautifying the same not a little.'

In the Convocation, which accepted the Articles in 1553, a committee of the House appears to have given a sanction to a catechism which had been drawn up by Poynet, Bishop of Winchester, and by him submitted to the King. The King, in his injunction giving authority to this catechism, says that it had been submitted 'to certain bishops and other learned men,' and appoints it to be taught by schoolmasters to their scholars. It was published first in Latin, with the Forty-two Arti-

Poynet's catechism

---

[1] See Lathbury's *History of Convocation*, p. 143, note x. An additional proof of the synodical acceptance of the Articles is furnished by a letter written by Sir John Cheke to Bullinger, where, speaking of the King, he says, 'Nuper articulos synodi Londinensis promulgavit;' *Two Liturgies*, Parker Soc., Preface, p. xii. Also John Clement, a martyr in the Marian persecution, says, in his Confession, 'I do accept, believe, and allow for a very truth all the godly articles that were agreed upon in the Convocation House, and published by the King's Majesty's authority in the last year of his most gracious reign.'—Strype, *Eccles. Memorials*, vol. iii. App. p. 210.

cles appended to it, and afterwards in English, with the Articles in English. This is called a 'Short Catechism,' but it is extremely verbose and tedious. The 'scholar' sermonises and argues, and the 'master' does not confine himself to asking questions, but runs into disquisitions. It formed the foundation of the still more verbose catechism of Alexander Nowel, from a synodical acceptance of which the Church of England only just escaped. The sacramental doctrine of this catechism is Zwinglian, its theology predestinarian.

The last of the manuals put forth in the reign of Edward VI. was the 'Primer, or Book of Private Prayer.' The publication of this book is another evidence of the triumph of the thoroughgoing reformers over the moderate party. In 1551 the King's Primer of 1545 had been reprinted with some alterations. But the book set out in 1553 was of altogether a different kind. It contains first the Calendar, then the Prayer-book Catechism, forms of grace at meals, directions for self-examination, a form of morning and evening prayer for each day, and a large body of special prayers, including prayers in behalf of judges, bishops, gentlemen, landlords, merchants, lawyers, labourers, rich men, poor men, masters, servants, &c., also prayers for the use of the several classes of worshippers, and petitions for various graces, &c. Some of the petitions are very singular compositions, and seem rather designed to instruct the Almighty than humbly to sue for His aid. Nothing could well be found more opposite to the style of the Prayer-book than this Primer, and it may be assumed as certain that Archbishop Cranmer had no share in its composition.

If in addition to these more formal and authorised documents we take into consideration the numerous writings of the chief reformers at this period, as Hooper's Declaration of Christ, Confession of Faith, Treatise on the Ten Commandments, and Exposition of some Psalms; Ridley's Treatise on the Lord's Supper, and the writings of many others of less note, it is evident that a sufficiently large amount of reformed teaching was now available for the instruction of the people. How far this instruction actually availed to correct the morals and raise the character of the people will be better judged after some other facts connected with this period have been detailed.

Writings of reformers

CHAPTER IX.

THE SECOND ENGLISH PRAYER-BOOK.
1552–1553.

It has been already remarked that a struggle between two parties, the moderate reformers and the thorough-going reformers, may be observed all through the reign of Edward VI. The former party is represented by the First Prayer-book. The latter obtained its triumph in the Second. The Primate belonged to the moderate section, and to a certain extent Bishop Ridley did also. It is remarkable that both Cranmer and Ridley opposed and protested against the bill for appointing thirty-two commissioners to draw up a new code of ecclesiastical law.[1]

[1] This may have been because only four bishops were named on the Commission.

THE SECOND ENGLISH PRAYER-BOOK 87

This scheme, which had its origin in the last reign, was now revived with a different meaning and intention than it had under Henry. The thirty-two Commissioners were in fact appointed, and drew up a scheme which we now know under the title of the *Reformatio legum ecclesiasticarum*. It failed, however, to receive the royal assent in this reign, and when revived in the days of Elizabeth failed also in like manner.

'Reformatio legum ecclesiasticarum'

And if Archbishop Cranmer was not eager for a sweeping change of the ancient canons, he was also little desirous of a change in the Liturgy which had so lately been established and vigorously enforced. In his work on the Eucharist he has left an emphatic testimony that he was fully satisfied with the service of the First Book. 'Thanks be to the Eternal God, the manner of the holy communion (which is now set forth in this realm) is agreeable with the institution of Christ, with St. Paul, and the old primitive and apostolic Church, with the right faith of the sacrifice of Christ upon the cross for our redemption, and with the true doctrine of our salvation, justification, and remission of our sins by that only sacrifice.' This was written about the beginning of the year 1550. The complaints against the First Prayer-book were first heard in Convocation towards the end of that year or the beginning of 1551. It is incredible that they could have proceeded from or been countenanced by the man who had thus written a short year before. Neither is there any reason to think that Bishop Ridley was dissatisfied with the first Liturgy. In his treatise on the Lord's Supper Ridley emphatically disclaims the opinion

Cranmer and Ridley satisfied with First Prayer-book

of those who make that sacrament only a bare sign or figure, and says: 'We deny the presence of Christ's body in the natural substance of His human and assumed nature, and grant the presence of the same by grace. By grace (I say) the same body of Christ is here present with us.' Ridley, therefore, cannot be classed with the Sacramentaries. It is true that he had been principally concerned in the movement against the ancient altars, which he thought to be incompatible with the reformed service. But, on the other hand, he was resolute for the retention of the episcopal vestments.

Who then was the leader of the movement against the English Liturgy which commenced to take formal proportions about the beginning of 1551?

John Hooper

Without doubt it was John Hooper. Hooper was perhaps the most remarkable man produced by the English Reformation. He was the stern, uncompromising, unsparing enthusiast. With him the altars were 'altars of Baal,' the priests who ministered at them 'priests of Baal.' Of the Liturgy he writes to Bullinger, 'The public celebration of the Lord's Supper is very far from the order and institution of our Lord.' In another passage, already quoted, he declares that he can never communicate according to the English book. He scoffs at Cranmer as 'too fearful about what may happen to him,' and at some of the other bishops as holding right views about the Lord's Supper, but 'kept back by the fear of their property from reforming their churches.' This enthusiast had resided seven or eight years abroad in the closest intimacy with Calvin, Bullinger, and the Swiss reformers. He had married a lady who was of their school, and he came into England at the beginning of the reign of Edward VI., fully determined in his own mind to strive to the uttermost for nothing less than a complete Swiss reformation. A treatise of his called 'A Declaration of Christ,' printed abroad and published immediately on his coming to England, with a dedication to the Duke of Somerset, made known his sentiments, and he soon became a popular and admired preacher. His views on the Eucharist were, as might be expected, simply those of the Swiss school. 'I believe it is a remembrance of Christ's death, a seal and confirmation of His precious body given unto death. It is a visible word that preacheth peace between God and man, exhorteth to mutual love and godly life.' The fall of the Protector Somerset resulted, not as was expected by many, in the triumph of the reactionary party, but rather in the triumph of the ultra-reformers. Somerset, with all his faults, had more care for the Church than Warwick, who succeeded him. Under the new influence Hooper was brought to preach a course of Lent sermons before the young King (1550). The boy King was very impressionable in the Puritan direction, and he no doubt now received a strong impulse towards seeking for further liturgical changes. In a short time (July 3) the fiery reformer was made Bishop of Gloucester. Hooper was quite willing to take a prominent post in the Church, but he scrupled at the necessary condition. He would neither wear the vestments, nor take the oath of Supremacy in which saints and angels were adjured. An attempt was made by the ultra-Protestant party to force the Bishop to yield, and to consecrate Hooper on his own terms. Had he done so, irreparable mischief might have happened to the Church of England. But Cranmer stood firm, and he carried the majority of the Council with him. He argued to no purpose with the stubborn Hooper. Bishop Ridley did the same. The opinions of Bucer and Martyr were brought to him to the effect that the vestments were not unlawful. Hooper would not yield, and was confined to his house and commanded not to publish anything. How far he obeyed this, an entry in the Council Book tells us (January 1, 1551). 'It appeared that Mr. Hooper had not kept his house, and that he had also written and printed a book wherein was contained matter that he should not have written, for the which, and for that also he persevered in his former opinion of not wearing the bishops' apparel, he was now committed to the Bishop of Canterbury's custody' (January 27). 'Upon letters from the Archbishop of Canterbury that Mr. Hooper cannot be brought to any conformity, but rather persevering in his obstinacy, *coveteth to prescribe orders and necessary laws of his head*, it was agreed that he should be committed to the Fleet.' Less than two months' durance in the Fleet served, however, to convince Hooper of the folly of resistance. He was consecrated in the full episcopal dress (March 8, 1551), and took the oath, the King having struck out with his own hand the clause which made mention of saints and angels. Hooper's entrance into Convocation was coincident with the first formal complaints against the Liturgy and service-book. Its opponents were able to appeal to the opinion of Calvin, who (as Collier says), 'continued still to intermeddle and solicit for his own fancy,' and to the long tirade of

Bucer, in which he blows hot and cold on the English Liturgy, with which Peter Martyr also agreed.

Things assumed a definite shape early in the year 1551. A committee was appointed, probably by Convocation, perhaps by an order from the King, to review the book. Some other matters were alleged to be needing change, but there is no question that it was against the communion office that the chief attack was directed. The Liturgy of the book of 1549 utterly refused to lend itself to the Zuinglian notion of a commemorative feast. In fact, it allowed a celebration very little differing from the old type of the mass service; especially when the 'Agnus Dei' was sung after the consecration and before the reception, which might well be treated as the worship of the divine presence in the elements. It also provided for the sacrificial character of the rite by the prayer for the descent of the Holy Spirit on the elements, the prayer of oblation, and the words used in the delivery of the elements. So nicely and with such judgment was the service balanced, that while Cranmer could praise it with enthusiasm (as has been seen), his great antagonist Gardiner could say of it: 'This holy mystery in the Book of Common Prayer is well termed, not distant from the Catholic faith in my judgment.' It was against these characteristics of the liturgical service, its recognition of the divine presence, and its sacrificial character, that the attacks of the extreme reforming party were directed. They had potent allies. The young King, who had been led to regard the mass as utterly hateful, declared that, if the bishops and divines would not make the required alterations, he would make them with his own hand,

Review of the First Prayer-book

and obtain the ratification of Parliament. Northumberland, and many other courtiers, eager for more church spoils, were anxious to lower as much as possible the ceremonial character of the services. The English divines may have saved their dignity by not making the alterations in the book in the way suggested by the foreign divines,[1] but that they made them in the direction which they pointed out is evident.

The second Communion Office, as it came forth from their hands, is of an entirely different character from the first. They altered the name, striking out the words 'commonly called the Mass;' they took away the ancient vestments and the introits; they introduced the recitation of the ten commandments with responses to signify the inward conditions required; they took away the prayer for the descent of the Holy Spirit and the oblation, the name of the blessed Virgin, the prophets and saints, the prayer for the dead, the manual acts, the signing the cross, the mixing of water with the wine, the Agnus Dei, making the reception follow immediately after the consecration; and most of all they removed the words used at the reception, and substituted a new form taken very nearly from the Liturgy used by John a Lasco. Thus the office was adapted so as to give no offence to the Sacramentaries, and was capable of being regarded simply as a sacred feast. The priest was now to stand at the north 'side of the table,' and not 'humbly afore the midst of the altar.' There was to be no oblation of the alms. They were to be deposited in the poor man's box.

The second Communion Office

[1] See Cardwell, Introduction to *Two Liturgies*, p. xxv.

The triumph of the thoroughgoing reformers was complete. The moderate party had yielded to them, doubtless for the sake of peace, and a new character was given for the moment to the worship of the Church of England. They were, however, far from being contented. There was still the solemn reception of the consecrated elements by kneeling worshippers, who might yet adore the divine presence even in the mutilated rite. The moderates had been ready to concede much, but they were not prepared entirely to revolutionise the service by abolishing the direction for kneeling. The extreme party then had recourse to another plan. Long after the book was agreed upon, six months after the Second Act of Uniformity, which legalised it, had become law, an order of Council was passed, explanatory of the posture of kneeling at the holy communion. Some impressions of the book had already been printed before this order was made, and in consequence do not contain it. In others it is found printed on a separate leaf, and thus bound into the book. Many alterations besides those in the communion service were made in the first service-book. Some of them were no doubt great improvements, as the exhortation, confession, and absolution at the beginning of matins, which were taken principally from the service-book of John a Lasco.

The Black Rubrick

The Second Act of Uniformity passed both Houses April 6, 1552. The moderate party were able to insert in it a handsome tribute to the merits of the First Book. It is described as 'a very godly order, agreeable to the word of God and the primitive church, very comfortable to all good people desirous to live

Second Act of Uniformity

in Christian conversation, and most profitable to the state of this realm'; and the new book is said to be put forth 'because there hath arisen in the use and exercise of the foresaid common service in the Church heretofore set forth divers doubts of the fashion and manner of the ministration of the same, rather by the curiosity of the minister and mistakers, than of any other worthy cause; therefore, for the more plain and manifest explanation hereof, as for the more perfection of the said order of common service, to make the same prayer and fashion of service more earnest and fit to stir Christian people to the true honouring of Almighty God,' &c. The book thus tenderly treated, and as to the calling in of which no order was given, probably remained in use in many churches. The use of the new book was to begin on All Saints' Day, 1552, and no doubt in the more prominent churches its use was then begun, as it was by Bishop Ridley at St. Paul's. But there is good reason to believe that it never became very generally used during the few months which intervened between All Saints' Day,[1] 1552, and the end of the reign of Edward VI.

[1] If the printing of the book was stopped for the introduction of the order in Council of October 27, very few copies could have been ready by All Saints' Day, November 1.

CHAPTER X.

THE LEGISLATION UNDER EDWARD VI.

1547-1553.

THE Reformation was doubtless mainly dependent for its progress on the formularies, manuals, and bodies of *Legislation of the first Parliament* instruction set forth by authority, or recommended by the position or power of the writers. But without the prop and stay of legislative acts it would have been very deficient in permanence and solidity. To obtain, therefore, a complete notion of what was done in the short reign of Edward VI. we need to attend to the progress of legislation.

The Parliament met November 4 (1547), and its first two acts relating to the holy communion and the appointment of bishops have been already mentioned. The third act was one of a most revolting character. It was directed against vagabonds, and from its numerous references to 'clerks convict,' the class of vagabonds specially intended was clearly the wandering 'religious,' who lived upon the alms of the people. The act allowed anyone to seize upon a 'vagabond,' carry him before a justice of the peace, have him branded with the letter V, and condemned to be a 'slave' for two years, to be fed on bread and water, and beaten and chastised as the master pleased. If the poor wretch attempted to escape, he was to be branded with S, and adjudged to be a slave for life. This act did not long continue to disgrace the statute book. It must, however, have served to make the governing body odious in the eyes of many, and to cast a slur upon the religious changes which they advocated. The act abolishing the treason statutes of Henry VIII. was altogether a wholesome one.

That which gave the King the property of colleges, free chapels, and chantries was a following out the precedents of the late reign, many of these foundations which had been granted to King Henry VIII. not having been taken possession of. The appetite for seizing upon the property of religious bodies, for the profit both of the State and individuals, had been created in the last reign, and could not now be easily appeased. Heylin writes: 'Though the Parliament consisted of such members as disagreed among themselves in respect of religion, yet they agreed well enough together in one common principle, which was to serve the present time and to preserve themselves. A great part of the nobility and not a few of the chief gentry in the House of Commons were cordially affected to the Church of Rome, yet were they willing to give way to all such acts and statutes as were made against it, out of a fear of losing such church lands as they were possessed of, if that religion should prevail and get up again.' The same writer observes that the hospitals, to the number of 110, were not included in this act, as they had been in that passed under Henry; but about ninety Colleges of Clerks (the Universities being excepted) and no fewer than 2,374 free chapels and chantries were vested in the King, for the purpose, as the Act states, of the maintenance of grammar schools and the support of preachers. Doubtless some portion of the spoil was thus applied; a

Act to give the King free chapels and chantries

The Legislation under Edward VI. 97

greater part probably fell into the hands of the courtiers.

Next session the Parliament legalised, somewhat grudgingly, the marriage of the clergy. Attention to
Marriage of clergy legalised the wording of this statute shows clearly that the Parliament was not much inclined towards reformation when there was no question of church spoils to be obtained. The preamble declares that it were much to be desired that priests and all others in holy orders might abstain from marriage; that thereby, being freed from the cares of wedlock and abstracted from the troubles of domestic business, they might more diligently attend the ministry, and apply themselves unto their studies. The Act nevertheless permits the marriage of priests, legalises the endowments of their wives, and makes their children heritable.

Another act, which reads as though it were an honest attempt to do justice to the clergy, was now passed.
Act for securing tithes By the change in the ecclesiastical system, the taking away of the power of the bishops, and the general disuse of excommunication (of which Bishop Latimer so bitterly complains), unscrupulous patrons and parishioners had in many cases been emboldened to divert to their own uses the monies accustomed to be paid to the clergy. There was no statute law which obliged them to pay the tithe, and the ecclesiastical law, which in old time had sufficed, was now greatly in abeyance. It was now enacted, that no person or persons should take away any tithes which had been received or paid within forty years next before the date of the act, or of right ought to have been paid, until he had divided the tenth part of the same,

or otherwise agreed with the incumbent or owner of the tithe, under penalty of forfeiting three times the amount. And in order to compensate the clergy for their loss by the cessation of offerings, it was enacted that personal tithes to the extent of a tenth of the profits made by anyone as a merchant, tradesman, or in any other art or faculty, should be payable to the clergy, and might be enforced by the ordinary. This last clause probably proved unworkable. A singular statute of the same session ordered abstinence from flesh in Lent and on other fasting days. In this act we may read a curious compromise. The Church party was gratified by having the old seasons of fasting recognised by law, while the reformers took out the sting of the concession by inserting in the act the objects of the restriction, namely, to preserve the breed of cattle, to promote health, and to encourage the fishermen.

In the autumn session the removal of all images and pictures of saints, except those upon tombs, was ordered. This had already been partially accomplished by injunction, but in many places the opposition, strenuously encouraged by Bishop Gardiner, was so strong that a statute with penalties was needed. In Cornwall one of the Visitors had been stabbed by the priest of the church while engaged in carrying out the work of removal. The unfortunate priest was afterwards hanged from the steeple of his own church.

Act for the removal of all images and pictures

The session of Parliament which passed the second Act of Uniformity engaged rather fully in ecclesiastical legislation. The act which sanctioned the observation of holidays is a very remarkable one. It is, as Heylin points out, distinctly anti-sabbatarian. It is well known that the earlier reformers, in their strong objections to all positive law, held somewhat lax notions as to the obligation of the Lord's Day. In this act the Sunday is placed on precisely the same footing as the other holidays. It asserts, 'There is no certain time nor definite number of days appointed by Holy Scripture, but the appointment of the time, as also of the days, is left to the liberty of Christ's Church by the Word of God; that the days which from henceforth were to be kept as holidays in the Church of England should be all Sundays in the year, the Feast of the Circumcision, the Epiphany, the Purification of the Blessed Virgin, with all the rest recited at the end of the Calendar in the public Liturgy; that the archbishop and bishops shall have the power to punish offenders, by the usual censures of the Church; that notwithstanding it shall be lawful for any husbandman, labourer, fisherman, &c., to labour, ride, fish, or work any kind of work on the foresaid holidays, not only in the time of harvest, but at any other time of the year when need shall require.' The eves of the holidays were also by this statute directed to be observed as fasts. The marriage of the clergy was now again legalised without the somewhat insulting qualifications which distinguished the first act. Further, a very severe act prohibited quarrelling and brawling in churches and churchyards; the use of a weapon in a consecrated place was subjected to the penalty of the loss of an ear.

Legislation of 1552, the Holidays Act

This act may be regarded as somewhat of a curiosity, for by this time the distinction between sacred and secular had been in a great measure obliterated. Service-books were sanctioned by acts of Parliament under the dread of secular penalties to be inflicted by the judges, while brawling, and refusing to contribute to the maintenance of the poor, were directed by the same authority to be visited by Church censures. In the midst of the convulsions and difficulties of this period—when new forms were displacing the old ones, and a multitude of new ideas were struggling to establish themselves as visible facts, when opposition to the efforts of the settling process was coming from many quarters at once, and statesmen knew not how to gauge public opinion, or in what direction to advance along the line of least resistance— it was to be expected that numerous anomalies would be found in the measures adopted both in Church and State. We might easily excuse this if principles were merely obscured, and for the moment forgotten. But it would be impossible to apologise on this ground for all that took place in matters relating to the Church during the reign of Edward VI. An organised system of selfish and unblushing spoliation of church property went forward, with but feeble opposition and condemnation. The leading statesmen were thoroughly unprincipled and selfish; the leading prelates too weak and ready with concessions. The young King, who had imbibed principles not altogether in accordance with the spirit of the Church of England, was yet a bright exception to those around him in the stedfastness with which he adhered to them. That the reader

Confusion between sacred and secular things

may judge the way in which the Church was handled at this period, some of the chief acts of spoliation and oppression will be brought together in the following chapter.

CHAPTER XI.

CHURCH SPOLIATION AND MORALS.

1547-1553.

IN estimating the spoliation of churches and the seizure by laymen of ecclesiastical property which were so prevalent at the period of the Reformation, it must not be forgotten that these practices were not the invention of those days. In the fourteenth and fifteenth centuries deliberate proposals were made to secularise the whole of the Church revenues. John Wycliffe maintained that this was permissible and might be desirable, and no one did more to establish the principle than some of the more energetic of the Popes. By collecting taxes from the clergy to carry on secular wars against the emperors, by authorising and enforcing church payments for King Henry III. to gain the kingdom of Sicily, the Popes of that period went far to obliterate the distinction between sacred and profane. It was not in the spirit of a doctrinal reformation that Wykeham, Waynflete, and Chichele used religious foundations for endowing secular colleges, or that Cardinal Wolsey and King Henry VIII. laid violent hands on the monastic property of their day, or that the latter spoiled the tomb of St. Thomas of its enormous treasure. Nor were the spoliations of the Reformation days confined to those who held reforming opinions. Queen Mary authorised the spoliation of churches as well as her brother, and consented to the retention of the abbey lands by those who had become possessed of them. It is not fair, therefore, to attribute the devastation of King Edward's days simply to the spirit of the Reformation. Rather it should be set down to the grasping, selfish, and unprincipled characters of the men who had the chief direction of affairs. Among these there was not one who redeemed his greed by any high qualities. Elizabeth's statesmen, it may be, were equally grasping; but they were at any rate men of powerful characters and great capacity for affairs. The leading bishops, as Cranmer, and especially Latimer, advocated some care for the temporal interests of the Church; but it must be confessed that their exhortations on this head were but little heeded.

The spoliation of the Church took many forms. There was first the pulling down of churches and ecclesiastical buildings to use the materials for secular building. Those who remembered the wholesale destruction of the fine abbeys under Henry VIII. would have little scruple about this. Then there was the robbing the sees of manors, which went on to a vast extent in the time of Edward VI., and was resumed under Elizabeth. There was also a very general retention of tithes from the lower clergy, the open sale of livings by the patron, and the promotion of obscure and unfit persons, on the understanding that they were only to receive a small part of the stipend. Lastly, there was the actual spoliation of churches, the

Various forms of Church spoliation

seizure of the vestments, the bells, the sacramental plate, for which purpose three several commissions were issued in the reign of Edward, and which was done, perhaps to a greater extent, by unauthorised spoilers.

Of the first sort of attack on church property the most notorious instance was the famous one of the erection of Somerset House. The Protector had at first deliberately intended to seize upon the noble Abbey of Westminster, and to pull it down for the erection of a palace on the site. Benson, the last abbot and first dean, hearing of the project, lost no time in offering an enormous bribe to save his church. But it needed the sacrifice of more than half the estates belonging to the foundation before the peril could be averted. Somerset then turned his attention to another site. 'He casts his eye upon a piece of ground in the Strand, on which stood three episcopal houses and one parish church; the parish church dedicated to the Virgin Mary, the houses belonging to the Bishops of Worcester, Lichfield, and Llandaff—all these he takes into his hands, the owners not daring to oppose, and, therefore, willingly assenting to it.' But the materials of the church and houses were not enough for the magnificent structure contemplated. An attempt was then made to seize St. Margaret's, Westminster; but this, being strenuously resisted, was abandoned. Somerset had to be content with a cloister of Old St. Paul's, and the rich work of the Church of St. John of Jerusalem—'most beautifully built not long before by Dockwray, a late prior thereof.' So arose Somerset House, although the unfortunate projector of it was not destined to enjoy the fair palace which he had planned.

This was but a sample of what was going on in every county of England when the Commissioners sent in March 1548 to carry out the act granting colleges and free chapels to the Crown were at work. The buildings were readily sold to neighbouring proprietors to be used as they thought fit. It was then that St. Stephen's Chapel became the Parliament House, and the famous College of St. Martin-le-Grand was turned into a tavern.

The Commissioners under the act for granting colleges, &c., to the King

As the houses of the nobility and gentry were built or enlarged from the churches, so were their estates swelled from the episcopal manors; for as the bishops now held their office at the will of the Crown, they were completely at the mercy of the State in regard to their property. The possessors of power did not fail to take full advantage of this. When Barlow, bishop of St. David's, was translated to Bath and Wells, he 'gratified the Lord Protector,' by a present of eighteen or nineteen manors, which, being situated in Somersetshire, were thought very appropriate to his title. 'There was no other means,' says Heylin, 'as the times then were, to preserve the whole, but by advancing some part thereof to the spoil of others.' Lord Wentworth obtained a fine property in London from the Dean and Chapter of St. Paul's; and Lord Paget, another courtier, seems to have been exceptionably fortunate in spoiling both the see of Exeter and that of Lichfield. To the former he owed a fine house, and to the latter the manor of Beau-desert, and 'many

Seizure of episcopal manors

other fair estates in the county of Stafford.' These last were surrendered, not by a newly-created bishop, but by one of old standing, who, being opposed to the reforming proceedings, found no other way to preserve his see. Bishop Sampson had played a conspicuous, and perhaps not over-honest, part in the reign of Henry VIII., and now found that royal supremacy, which he had done his best to exaggerate, an inconvenient power in his own case. Salcot, bishop of Salisbury, avoided the actual surrender of his manors by making long leases of them. But Kitchen, bishop of Llandaff, was less scrupulous. His see was so richly endowed that it might be reckoned one of the most wealthy in Christendom; but by his grants it was so impoverished 'that it is hardly able to keep the pot boiling for a parson's dinner.' When Voysey, bishop of Exeter, was implicated in the Devonshire rebellion, the greater part of the endowments of his see were forfeited, which once consisted of twenty-two goodly manors and fourteen mansion-houses. Upon the accession of Poynet to the see of Winchester, after the deprivation of Gardiner, that rich see was severely amerced, though the manors and palaces seized upon by the courtiers were afterwards recovered on the restoration of Gardiner. When Bishop Heath was removed from Worcester, this see was given to Hooper, bishop of the new diocese of Gloucester, to hold in commendam. But he only held the see as administrator, its revenues being grasped by the 'pirates of the Court.' Thus the impoverishment of the sees went on throughout all the dioceses of England. The legal pretence was an act of Henry VIII., which enabled bishops to exchange manors for impropriate tithes that had come into the King's hands; but there is no evidence of an equivalent having been given at this time. The spoliation of the wealthy see of Durham was obtained by the Duke of Northumberland, through the attainder of Bishop Tonstal, on pretence of being implicated in a rising in the north. This good bishop, together with Gardiner, Bonner, Heath, Day, and Voysey, remained in prison till the accession of Queen Mary. The strangest disregard of ecclesiastical rights prevailed throughout all this period. Crumwell had been dean of Wells under Henry VIII. Somerset held not only a deanery, but also a treasurership and four cathedral prebends.

But if the bishops were heavily amerced, they still had some revenues left. This, however, in numerous instances was not the case with the parochial clergy. A very large proportion of the benefices of England had in the course of the middle ages passed into the hands of the monasteries, which had been compelled, both by ecclesiastical and statute law, to appoint as permanent vicars, clerks outside their body at a fixed stipend, or, when the monastic house was clerical, to serve the churches by one of their own body. Thus the Benedictines, Cistercians, the military orders, and all houses of nuns appointed vicars; the Austin canons, and other foundations of canons, usually served the church themselves. When then, at the dissolution of monasteries, these impropriate tithes passed into lay hands, the same duties devolved on the holders of them, as regards the churches, as had belonged previously to the religious house. There is an

Spoliation of benefices

unanimous testimony from contemporary writers, that these duties were performed very inadequately or were altogether evaded. A contemporary writer says, 'Where the monks always had one or other vicar that either preached or hired some one to preach, now there is no vicar at all; but the farmer is vicar and parson altogether, and an old castaway monk or friar that can scarcely say his matins, is hired for twenty or thirty shillings, meat and drink, yea, in some places for meat and drink alone, without wages.' Bishop Latimer thus addresses the patrons of benefices: 'What do you patrons? Sell your benefices, or give them to your servants for their service, for keeping of hounds, or hawks, for making of your gardens. These patrons regard no souls, neither their own nor other men's. To consider what hath been plucked from abbeys, colleges, and chantries, it is marvel no more to be bestowed on this holy office of salvation. Many will choose now such a curate for their souls as they may call fool, rather than one that will rebuke their covetousness, ambition, unmercifulness, uncharitableness.' In older times the bishop had full power to force an augmentation of the vicar's stipend, when it was shown to be insufficient. Now the bishops were powerless, and the lay patrons had it all their own way. The vicar's stipend was often withheld altogether, and where perpetual curacies were established, which was done in those cases where the church had been served directly from the monastery, there was no check upon the bargain which might be made between the patron and any compliant priest he might be able to find. In addition to this, it appears that many rectorial incumbents had, like the bishops, alienated the manors and lands belonging to their benefices.

Poverty was thus threatening the Church on all sides, nor were the sacred edifices and their contents spared. The Government proceeded on the theory that church ornaments and vestures, not needed for the performance of service according to the new settlement, belonged to the Crown, and were to be kept for its use. With this view commissions to take inventories had been issued in the earlier part of the reign, but it does not appear that the goods inventoried had been removed. As the reforming spirit, however, developed itself, it seems that a great quantity of private pillage of church valuables was experienced. Accordingly in 1553 a new commission was issued, the duty of which was to obtain the inventories which were in the hands either of the clerk of the peace or the bishop, and to compare the lists with the articles found in each church; where any of them were missing the commissioners were to trace out the purloiner, and if possible to recover the lost article. But the commissioners were to do more than this. Their principal duty is euphoniously expressed thus:—' They shall give good charge and order that the same goods, and every part thereof, be at all times forthcoming to be answered.' No way appeared so satisfactory for effecting this as that of removing them from the churches altogether, and that this was intended appears from the next sentence, 'leaving nevertheless in every parish church or chapel of common resort—one, two, or more chalices or cups, according to the multitude of the people in every such church or chapel, and also such other ornaments as by their discretion shall seem requisite for the divine service in every such place for the time.' A very large number of the returns made by these commissioners remains among the Augmentation Office papers, many of which have been printed as curiosities of the time. The following, taken from the return for a deanery in the diocese of Norwich, may serve as specimens:—

Church 1.

	£	s.	d.
1 chalice parcel gilt, with paten of silver parcel gilt weighing 9½ ounces, at 3s. 4d. per ounce	1	14	10
1 cope of cloth of Bawdekin	0	6	8
1 vestment of green sarsnet	0	2	0
1 cross of copper	0	4	9
2 bells weighing 9 cwt., at 15s. the cwt.	6	15	0

The following were assigned for divine service—The chalice, 1 surplice, 2 tablecloths, 1 bell.

Church 2.

	£	s.	d.
1 chalice parcel gilt weighing 11¼ ounces, at 3s. 4d. the ounce	2	8	9
1 chalice of silver weighing 2 ounces	0	6	8
1 cope blue silk	0	4	0
1 vestment blue silk, with the alb	0	3	0
1 old cope of green say	0	1	0
1 vestment white fustian	0	1	0
1 cross, 1 pair censers of latten	0	0	4
2 handbells 8 lb.	0	1	0
3 bells in steeple 18 cwt.	13	10	0
3 clappers (whereof two do remain in the hands of Sir Anthony Hevingham, Knt.)	0	3	4

The following assigned for divine service—The chalice, 1 surplice, 1 bell.

Bells were evidently the principal spoil. The copes and vestments were but of little value, as no doubt there were many who would shrink from putting them to profane uses. It is remarkable that, though the chalice was usually assigned to the church, the paten was ordinarily carried away. It appears to be thought that any ordinary plate might suffice. The cathedrals probably fared as badly, perhaps worse, than the parish churches. The primate, though a member of the Council, could not protect his own church. January 16, 1548, occurs in the Council books the following: 'A letter to the Dean and Prebendaries of Canterbury to deliver the silver table that stood upon their high altar, by indenture containing the weight of the same, to Sir Anthony Aucher.' January 29: 'To Mr. Aucher to receive of the Chapter of Christ Church in Canterbury, all such jewels and plate of gold and silver as they have by their late sovereign lord's permission to their church's use, and forthwith to deliver the same by bill indented to the officers of the Mint.' In these various ways the Church was spoiled during this period.

It would be unfair to forget among these selfish graspings that the young King himself showed an altogether different spirit. From the sale of chantry and free-chapel lands twenty-two grammar-schools were founded, and just at the end of his life the King made considerable benefactions to the City of London. He gave the palace of Bridewell to be a place of relief for travellers and correction for the idle and vagabond. He dissolved the Hospital of the Savoy and gave its revenues to the Hospitals of

St. Thomas, St. Bartholomew, and Christ Church; the buildings of which on the destruction of the religious houses had been rescued by the City of London from the grasp of the King. Thus Christ's Hospital became a noble free school, and the others became institutions of infinite value for the sick and suffering. If King Edward did not do more with the Church property which came into his possession, it was certainly the fault of his advisers rather than his own. In many ways the young King was infinitely superior to his surroundings.

This was especially marked in the melancholy case of the woman Joan Boucher, who was condemned to
Burning of Joan Boucher death in 1549, for some mad blasphemies as to the Incarnation of our Lord. For a whole year this woman was kept in prison, and the greatest efforts were made by Cranmer and others to make her recant. She obstinately refused, and at length a warrant was made out for her burning. It needed, however, all Cranmer's emphatic declarations, and his assertion that he took the sole responsibility upon himself, before the young King could be induced to yield to the barbarous spirit of the age. The poor creature was burned May 2, 1550. One other execution for heresy only, that of George Van Parre, an Anabaptist, took place in this reign.

It is hard, almost impossible, to estimate the relative amounts of immorality prevailing in society at
The morality of the period different periods; but there is a general consent that in the times of Edward VI. all moral obligations were greatly loosened. Something of this might naturally be expected from the state of

chaos in which religious matters were, and from the relaxation of the old bonds of Church authority, while as yet the secular government was not strong or energetic enough to redress disorders. Camden's estimate is :—' That ambition and faction amongst the nobility, insolence and insurrection among the commons, were never more flagrant or disturbing. In short, considering the animosities and tumults amongst great men, the debasing the coin, the disorders in the administration and the revolt of the peasantry, the kingdom made a miserable appearance, and looked as it were languishing in one part and distracted in another.' In the singular rhodomontades which Bishop Latimer delivered as sermons, the most violent attacks are constantly made upon the wickedness of the age. But this is a commonplace with all preachers, and it is hard to gather anything definite as to the state of society from such words. Whatever it may have been, the religious Reformation cannot fairly be held accountable for it. As yet this was scarcely inaugurated; and all things were in an unfinished and chaotic state, when the young King died at Greenwich (July 6, 1553), and men's hearts were filled with anxiety and fear as to the prospect before them in a new reign.

CHAPTER XII.

THE FIRST MEASURES OF RETALIATION.

1553-1554.

BY the accession of Mary to the throne after the short and melancholy episode of Lady Jane Grey, the whole aspect of affairs in the English Church was completely changed. The situation was in some respects parallel to that in the time of Henry VIII., when the King suddenly drew back from the reforming party, and by the passing of the Six Article Law and the disgrace of Crumwell, struck terror into those who desired further reforms. Without contending for an exact parallel, it is nevertheless true that both these sanguinary checks to the progress of the Reformation were made to subserve good and useful purposes. Another year or two of the power of King Edward's counsellors, and it is probable that but little of the face of the ancient Church of England would have been left. There might have been a Directory in place of the Prayer-book, and the call of the congregation instead of ordination by the Bishop. But there came a terrible time of trial. The Reformed Church was baptized in blood. The halo of martyrdom was spread around it. The enthusiasm of men was stirred. Their hearts were touched. The most intense feelings of horror for the opposing system were generated, and to this day the Queen who was the cause of the cruelties

Change by the accession of Mary

which were practised is regarded with dislike by the mass of Englishmen.

There is much excuse to be made for Mary. She had been persecuted more or less all her life, as her mother had been before her. She had been most unjustifiably vexed and annoyed as to her religious observances during the late reign. The Reformation and all its supporters could not be anything but absolutely odious to her. She was much more of a Spanish than an English woman. She had altogether the Spanish temperament; short and slightly made, but with a saturnine look and a deep voice, she was absolutely unyielding in obstinacy, and entirely devoid of fear. She knew nothing of the feelings of pity and compassion. She was sternly determined to do what she believed to be her duty. In doing this she scrupled not to use falsehood. Her most honoured counsellor was her cousin the Emperor Charles V., and he has left it on record that no faith ought to be kept with heretics, and that he bitterly repented not having broken his word and put Luther to death when he was in his power. Calvin called her Proserpine, as having all the qualities suitable for reigning in Hell. The English nation has agreed to affix to her name another epithet, from which it will probably never shake itself free. For it is now known, almost with certainty, that it was not to the politic Gardiner, nor to the coarse and butcherly Bonner, nor to the amiable Pole, nor to any of the English bishops, that the cruelties of this reign were mainly due; but to the vindictive temper of the Queen herself, encouraged and approved by the cold-blooded murderous principles of her husband.

Character of the Queen

THE FIRST MEASURES OF RETALIATION 115

The first ecclesiastical act of Mary's reign was one which all would naturally expect. Bishop Gardiner was set free from the Tower, Bonner from the Marshalsea, and Tonstal from the King's Bench prison. Bishops Voysey, Day, and Heath were also liberated, and the holders of their sees, Poynet, Ridley, Coverdale, Scory, and Hooper, were dispossessed. This appears to have been done by a Commission appointed by the Council, which also deprived all deans, dignitaries, and parochial ministers who had during the last two reigns succeeded to any preferment of which the old incumbent was still living.

Release of the imprisoned bishops

Heylin says 'the people were generally well affected to the Reformation.' There is, however, very little trace of this. There was a general acquiescence in what came to be called 'The Queen's Proceedings.' The old services were soon seen everywhere, though still illegal; and we can hardly wonder at the caustic observations of the Venetian Ambassador, who writes, 'The example and authority of the Sovereign are everything with the people of this country in matters of faith. As he believes, they believe. Judaism or Mahometanism is all one to them. They conform themselves easily to his will, at least so far as the outward show is concerned, and most easily of all where it concerns their own pleasure and profit.'

Indifference of the people

There was, however, some spirit of resistance in the Parliament, which met October 5. It would not repeal the Acts on religion passed under Henry VIII., nor would it express its desire that the Queen should marry the Spanish Prince. It was with very great difficulty that it was brought to annul the Acts

Resistance of the Parliament

on religion of Edward VI., about a third of the assembly standing out for the Reformation settlement; but it was at length agreed that the form of Divine Service and Administration of the Sacraments which were used in the last year of King Henry VIII., should henceforth be the legal service, and no other.

In the Convocation there was not so stout a resistance to the changed state of religious affairs as in the Parliament. Only five divines—Phillips, Dean of Rochester, Cheyney, Archdeacon of Hereford, Haddon, Dean of Exeter, Philpot, Archdeacon of Winchester, and Aylmer, Archdeacon of Stow[1]— ventured to dispute openly against resolutions which reaffirmed in the most pointed manner the doctrine of Transubstantiation and the sacrifice of the Mass. It is said that the proctorial elections were so managed that none of 'King Edward's clergy,' as they were termed, were sent to the House, those who defended the reforming doctrines being all dignitaries. Of course their opposition was overruled, the Prolocutor closing the discussion with very remarkable words: 'It is not the Queen's pleasure that we should spend any more time in these disputes, and ye are well enough already, for you have the word, and we have the sword.'

The Convocation of Canterbury

Nothing indeed could better describe the state of affairs than these words. The 'Queen's Pleasure,' was now to be the absolute law for the Church, as in the days of Henry VIII. She put out a proclamation forbidding preaching. She issued a set of injunctions, as 'Head of the Church,' to the bishops, bidding them deprive the married clergy, re-establish

Exercise of the Royal Supremacy

[1] There is said to have been a sixth, whose name is not known.

the ancient services and processions, set forth Homilies; and by Commissions appointed under the authority of the Crown, she caused all the reforming bishops, on one ground or other, to be deprived. Only Cranmer, being a Metropolitan and having been appointed by Papal Bulls, could not be thus dealt with without direct authority from Rome.

This, no doubt, was Bishop Gardiner's policy. Cardinal Pole, designed to be the Papal Legate in England, would have acted differently. But Pole, on Gardiner's advice, was kept back, by the Emperor's influence. Had he appeared in England at once, and before the Abbey lands were secured to their lay-holders, it was thought to be not improbable that the Queen would lose her Crown. The Queen's advisers as yet had no thought of persecution other than that which had been used in the last reign. Then the romanizing bishops had been deprived and sent to prison; now, the same measure was meted out to the reforming bishops. Some of them, indeed, as Barlow, Poynet, and Coverdale, escaped. A great number of the inferior clergy and of the lay folk who were most in earnest about the Reformation followed their example. The foreigners had all been allowed to pass freely. Gardiner, foreseeing probably troubles ahead, was glad to be rid of them. It is said that even Archbishop Cranmer had an opening for escape; but this seems scarcely credible. Against him more than any other man the Queen nourished a deadly hatred. In her view, he had misled her father, pronounced the divorce of her mother, overturned the mass, and brought persecution upon her for her religion during her brother's

Gardiner's policy

reign. All this had been aggravated by his endeavour to set her aside in favour of Lady Jane Grey. Cranmer, under one pretext or another, must needs be sacrificed. Gardiner would probably have been satisfied with his deprivation. He bore the Primate no good-will, and besides, he wanted his place; but Pole was a formidable rival. Could not, perhaps, Pole be kept out altogether, or, at any rate, for some time? Certainly this could not be done unless some measures were taken against the leading heretics. The Queen's impatience for revenge could not otherwise be met.

So a singular resolve was taken. Cranmer, Ridley, and Latimer were sent to Oxford (March 1554). Hooper, Rogers, Philpot, Bradford, Crome and Taylor were reserved for Cambridge. There was to be a great academical discussion on the doctrine of the mass, in which the heretics were to be ignominiously worsted. What was to be done with them afterwards had not as yet been decided upon. At Oxford the controversial duel took place in St. Mary's Church (April 14, 16, 17, 20). The bishops defended their opinions with great zeal; but they were interrupted, howled at, mobbed, and of course condemned to be guilty of heresy. This, however, was merely an academical resolution, which hurt nobody, and perhaps this was all that Gardiner desired. But it by no means satisfied the Queen. At the beginning of May the Judges and Queen's Counsel were summoned to be asked what might be done against the heretical bishops. There was a considerable difficulty. The Act 25 Henry VIII., c. 16, had repealed the old Lollard Laws, and substituted another process. The Six Article Law

Measures against the reforming bishops

had made heresy a statutable offence; but the Six Article Law had been repealed under Edward, and had not been re-enacted. There was nothing for it but to wait for better times, until the Legate should come, with full power to assure the holders of Church spoils that they would not be disturbed, and then a repentant and grateful Parliament would doubtless cheerfully re-enact the Lollard Laws. Gardiner has left it on record that he disapproved of this policy, and we may readily believe him. Shifty and unprincipled as he was, he yet was English, and did not thirst for blood. In his predilections he was anti-papal. He was quite satisfied to work the Royal Supremacy, for which he had learnedly argued in the days of Henry VIII., and he had no desire for the Spaniard and the Inquisition. The retaliation which had been already meted out to the prominent Reformers probably satisfied him, and had Cranmer been duly deposed, and he himself substituted in his room, his appetite for revenge would have been fully appeased. But behind and above him there was a very different spirit, fostered and upheld by influences which are now to be detailed. Before this his power waned and fell, while the influence which overcame him availed to write the saddest and most humiliating chapter in the whole history of England.

CHAPTER XIII.

THE SPANISH REVENGE.

1554-1558.

ON July 25, 1554, Queen Mary was married, at Winchester, to a prince who was the most perfect type and embodiment of cold-blooded cruelty. He had been educated in the notion that to burn or otherwise destroy heretics was the most acceptable piacular offering to heaven; and in this spirit he is found showing his gratitude for preservation in a storm by extemporising an auto-da-fé, or at another time causing twenty-seven gentlemen convicted of heresy to be burned in his presence. When Philip came to England he did not come alone. With him there came Bartholomeo de Carranza, who had represented Spain at the Council of Trent, and who was afterwards Archbishop of Toledo; Pedro de Soto, Confessor to Charles V.; Juan de Villagarcia, and some other Dominicans.[1] Philip also brought with him as his chaplain Alphonso de Castro, a Franciscan.

In the 'Life of Carranza' it is stated, 'As it was the intention of the affianced parties to reduce the kingdom of England to the unity and bosom of the Catholic Church, the enterprise was begun by Carranza receiving orders to pass over into England, and to take with him great and learned clerks who might arrange the business dexterously, conquer-

The Spanish divines

Bartholomeo de Carranza

---

[1] One of these, Constantine Ponce, became converted to reforming views in England, and was afterwards condemned by the Inquisition.

The Spanish Revenge

ing the difficulties which might present themselves.' Carranza became the Queen's confessor, and was employed in the visitation of both the universities. To him is to be set down one of the most infamous acts of the 'revenge,' namely, the disinterring and burning the bodies of Fagius and Bucer, and the burying the remains of Peter Martyr's wife in a dunghill. For this he himself takes credit. It is probable also, from some expressions of his, that he attempted to induce the Queen to establish the Inquisition in England, for which, if it were so, a strange nemesis overtook him, for he passed the last sixteen years of his life in the dungeons of the Holy Office.

Pedro de Soto was made Regius Professor at Oxford in succession to Peter Martyr. He was doubtless considered the man most calculated to undo the mischief of the reforming teaching of his predecessor. Having been long confessor to the Emperor Charles, he had left him and established himself in Flanders with the special object of confuting the German heresies. From this he had been drawn into England as a yet more promising field for his labours; and at Oxford he 'reinstated the theology of St. Thomas, the solid buttress against heretics, and banished their fictitious and fallacious doctrine.'

Pedro de Soto

Villagarcia, another Dominican, also sent to Oxford, and appointed to a professorship, was a member of the Convent of St. Paul, at Valladolid. He had obtained high reputation in his own country, and is said by Fernandez 'to have been taken to England to purify the universities of that realm of the views which the heretic doctors had sown in them. He laboured

Villagarcia

indefatigably in scattering the darkness with which the Lutheran and Calvinist teachers had blinded the students.' He is said to have read theological lectures both at Lincoln and Magdalen Colleges. All these divines will be found to have been employed around the unfortunate Archbishop Cranmer, in carrying out the scheme of refined malice devised against him, namely, to make him first recant and deny his former teaching, and then to burn him in spite of his recantation.

But the most remarkable of the Spaniards who at this time alighted upon the unfortunate Church of England was Alphonso de Castro, 'King Philip's preacher.' He is remarkable in this, that whereas the others did not stoop to dissemble their horrible maxims of fire and sword for heretics, De Castro, for politic reasons and at the instance of his master, actually ventured to preach a sermon in which he denounced vindictive proceedings against heretics, endeavouring to throw the odium of these inhumanities upon the English bishops, and to gain for the Spaniard the praise of mercy. With this apparatus of divines the Spanish prince came to England. The effect of his arrival, and the support which he and his clergy lent to the Queen's vindictive temper, was soon apparent in the complete downfall of Gardiner's policy, and the commencement of a new state of things.

Alphonso de Castro

In November (1554) arrived Cardinal Pole, being the bearer of a Bull from the Pope, empowering him to alienate and transfer to its present holders all the monastic and church property which had been granted or sold to laymen. This welcome document insured the Cardinal's favourable

Arrival of the Papal Legate and absolution of the nation

reception. Parliament first, and then the Convocation of the Clergy, were quite ready to receive with due expressions of gratitude and humility the absolution sent to them from the Pope. The dispensation was at once embodied in an Act of Parliament, which recited the return of the English nation to the papal obedience, and confirmed the settlement of cathedrals and schools, marriages celebrated, and institutions to benefices during the schismatical period. The clergy were sent home from their synod with a direction to use lenity, and a form of absolution was furnished them for the reconciling of their flocks. The Parliament, in the spirit of zeal and gratitude produced by the confirmation of the titles to the confiscated Church lands, repealed the Act of Henry VIII., which made the trial of heretics difficult, and revived the statutes made against the Lollards.

This was done in December; but fully a month before this and before the arrival of the Cardinal, the Queen, in anticipation of the policy resolved upon by herself and her Spanish friends, had addressed to the Council her famous letter in which she gives her regulations for the punishment of heretics. 'Specially within London,' she writes, 'I would wish none *to be burnt* without some of the Council's presence, and both there and everywhere good sermons at the same time.' The Queen, therefore, now married about four months, had already decided to burn a considerable portion of her subjects, even before her Roman adviser had arrived. What was her motive? Everything was quiet in England. No danger threatened from abroad. The leading Reformers had either fled or were in prison. The

The Queen's determination to burn

bishops were making no demands for violent measures. The Queen had been tranquilly settled on her throne for more than a year, and yet a preparation was being made for a great burning, with 'good sermons' to edify the people. Here then was a complete demonstration of the triumph of Spanish ideas and Spanish principles. The unhappy English bishops were, however, to be made the instruments. Gardiner, who completely detested this policy, avowed, at the examination of Rogers, that 'the Queen went before them in those counsels which proceeded of her own proper motion.'

On January 29 (1555), the Cardinal Legate issued his Commission to Bishops Gardiner, Tonstal, Capon, Thirlby, and Aldridge, to proceed to the trial of heretics. Of these five Commissioners it may be said with certainty that three at least—Gardiner, Tonstal, and Aldridge—were opposed to persecution. Thirlby and Capon were shifty prelates who had bought toleration during the last reign by the sacrifice of manors; but there is no reason to believe that they were bloodthirsty. In fact, there is no English prelate of the day to whom this character can fairly be attributed, except perhaps Bonner. Bonner did not originate the persecution, but he seems to have entered into it heartily; and the brutal way in which he treated the married clergy in his diocese may lead one to suspect that he could even take pleasure in the cruelties of which he was the instrument. Before the Episcopal Commissioners sitting at St. Mary Overy Church, Southwark, were brought from their prison, Rogers, Prebendary of St. Paul's, and Hooper, late Bishop of Gloucester.

The first Commission

Hooper had been the leader of the extreme reforming party in the late reign; and that uncompromising spirit which had led him to condemn unhesitatingly everything which he thought savoured of superstition, did not now desert him. He had been scandalously ill-treated in the Fleet prison, 'having nothing appointed to him for his bed but a little pad of straw, and a rotten covering with a tick and a few feathers therein, the chamber being vile and stinking. On the one side the sink and filth of the house, and on the other the Tower ditch, so that the stench of the house infected him with divers diseases.' During the time he was sick he 'had mourned, called, and cried for help, but in vain.' On his appearing, Gardiner made an earnest attempt to induce him to submit and receive the Pope's blessing, as he himself had done; but all in vain. After a second examination, being adjudged to be guilty of heresy, he was delivered over to the sheriffs. In pursuance of the policy which had been determined on, it was arranged that Hooper should suffer at his late cathedral city, and he was consequently escorted to Gloucester, riding joyfully and merrily to the goal which he ardently desired. The details of his execution are too shocking to be dwelt upon. The inefficient fire, which consumed only his lower extremities, gave him three-quarters of an hour of intense agony, but the brave spirit of the man never quailed. He continued to pray until prayer was no longer possible and no longer needed. The execution of Rogers was of a similar character. The French Ambassador notes that the people were so delighted at his constancy, 'that they did not fear to strengthen his courage by their acclamations, even his own children joining and consoling him after such a fashion that it seemed as though they were conducting him to his nuptials.'

Dr. Rowland Taylor, parson of Hadley, in Suffolk, was a man in high repute for learning, but more remarkable as a parish priest, and so diligent in his work 'that the whole town seemed rather an university of the learned than a town of clothmaking and labouring people.' Soon after the accession of Mary some restless spirits endeavoured to introduce into the parish 'The Queen's Proceedings,' and brought a neighbouring parson to say Mass in the church. This Dr. Taylor stoutly resisted, upon which he was apprehended and brought before the Lord Chancellor, Gardiner. After the usual amount of browbeating and rude talk, Taylor was committed to the King's Bench prison, where he seems to have been better treated than Bishop Hooper was. He was soon afterwards deprived of his benefice for being married, and after nearly two years' imprisonment was brought before the Commissioners in Southwark. Gardiner spoke at first kindly to him and endeavoured to induce him to yield; but he defended his opinions with great spirit, and when it was perceived that nothing could be done with him, he was handed over to the sheriff to be burned in his own parish of Hadley. The admirable temper and constancy with which he met his fate was the most effective of sermons to the people; and it must have been soon apparent to those who managed these proceedings, that there could not have been a more mistaken policy than to arrange the execution of these

THE SPANISH REVENGE 127

sufferers in the places where they were most known and reverenced. They thus gave them the opportunity of sealing and confirming their teaching in a way that could not be mistaken, and invested their doctrines with a sanctity which could not fail to promote their spread. It is probable that the Reformation went forward more rapidly and with more real power in the days of Mary than it had done in those of King Edward.

To some of the prisoners very great liberty was permitted, which they did not fail to use for the teach-
ing of the people. We are told of Bradford, Prebendary of St. Paul's, that 'for the time he did remain prisoner he preached twice a day continually, unless sickness hindered him; where also the Sacrament was often administered, and through his means (the keepers so well did bear with him) such resort of good folks was daily to his lecture, and to the ministration of the Sacrament, that commonly his chamber was well-nigh filled.' This good man was so trusted by his keepers that they even allowed him to ride into Oxfordshire, being certain that he would keep faith with them. Bradford, when condemned to the stake, suffered with a constancy equal to those who had preceded him, his companion in suffering being an apprentice lad named Leaf, who imitated his example of fortitude. Bradford's execution was deferred till July (1555), but another of the earlier batch of martyrs who suffered in February ought not to be passed over.

John Bradford

This was Laurence Saunders, Rector of All Hallows, Bread Street, first committed by Bonner for alleged heresy on the Eucharist, and in January (1555) brought before the Commissioners. The feelings of some of the bishops could not have been very pleasant when this brave man said to them, in reply to a reproach that he was 'dividing himself by singularity from the Church'—'For dividing myself from the Church, I live in the faith wherein I have been brought up since I was fourteen years old; being taught that the power of the Bishop of Rome is but usurped, with many other abuses springing thereof. Yea, this I have received, *even at your hands that are here present*, as a thing agreed upon by the Catholic Church and public authority.' To this there seems to have been no answer; and as Gardiner, Bonner, and Tonstal had taught precisely the same when it was their interest to do so, an answer would have been difficult. With the same mistaken policy which had sent Hooper to Gloucester and Taylor to Hadley, Saunders was sent to suffer at Coventry, where he had formerly held preferment.

[margin: Laurence Saunders]

On March 30 Farrar, Bishop of St. David's, an eccentric man who pleased neither party, and was actually in prison at the death of King Edward, was condemned by his successor in the see, and burned at Carmarthen. This was a new element of horror. A shudder was running throughout the land, and it was seen that there was a danger of reaction. Gardiner and Tonstal abandoned their places on the Commission, and would act no more in this bloodthirsty business.

[margin: Bishop Farrar]

It was then that Alphonso de Castro was put up to preach his famous sermon, in which he advocated lenity and gentle dealing with heretics. But how much reality there was about this was soon to be shown.

[margin: Sermon of Alphonso de Castro]

At the end of May the Council addressed a letter to the Bishops, reproving them for their slackness, and bidding them proceed against those who were suspected of heresy. This at any rate seems to have stirred up Bishop Bonner. In June six persons were burned at Smithfield, five of them being mechanics. As victims must be found to satisfy the Queen and the Spaniards, it was easier to secure them from the unlettered class, whose powers of disputation were small, than from such acute disputants as Taylor, Bradford, and Saunders. So Bonner went on making havoc of the poor creatures in his diocese, committing to the flames during the reign of Mary no less than 128 persons. As the year went on, the fires were kindled in various places, especially at Canterbury, where no less than eighteen persons were burned.

The Bishops checked for slackness

But when September came the attention of all men was fixed upon Oxford, where after two years' detention in the prison called Bocardo, the three most illustrious of the Reformers, Cranmer, Ridley, and Latimer, were to be tried by a legatine Commission. Though they had been joined together in the disputation, yet now they must be treated differently. Cranmer, as a Metropolitan, appointed by Papal Bulls, must needs be sentenced directly from Rome; with Latimer and Ridley the Cardinal's Commissioners—the Bishops of Lincoln, Gloucester, and Bristol were competent to deal. On September 30, in the Divinity School at Oxford, articles were given to them, which they were to answer. The next day in St. Mary's Church the answers were received. The accused were then pronounced to be heretics, and

Ridley and Latimer

ordered to be degraded and excommunicated. It was the same wretched story as in all these ghastly doings. The Sacrament of love and mercy was made the pretence for dragging venerable men, even those in extreme old age, as was Latimer, to the agonies of the stake. The Bishop of Lincoln, the president of the Commission, spoke very courteously to Ridley, and exhorted him earnestly to recant. 'Remember,' he said, 'Master Ridley, you were once one of us. You have taken degrees in the school. You were made a priest and became a preacher, setting forth the same doctrine that we do now. In a sermon of yours at Paul's Cross you as effectually and as catholicly spake of that blessed Sacrament as any man might have done. I wish you to return thither from whence you came, that is, together with us to acknowledge the truth, to acknowledge the Church of God, to acknowledge the supremacy of our most reverend father in God, the Pope's Holiness.' Ridley answered everything with the greatest calmness. As regards his sermon at Paul's Cross, he said that many irreverent attacks upon the Sacrament of the Lord's Supper were abroad, and so he 'preached as reverently of that matter as he might, declaring what estimation and reverence ought to be given to it, what danger ensued the mishandling thereof, affirming in that Sacrament to be truly and verily the body and blood of Christ effectuously by grace and spirit.' And yet the man who held this doctrine was to suffer death as a heretic in the matter of the Eucharist. 'I prefer the antiquity of the primitive Church,' said the Bishop, 'before the novelty of the Church of Rome;' and for this he must die.

Bishop Latimer, old and broken as he was, exhibited before the Commissioners a true dignity, and spoke with much pathos and power. 'I acknowledge,' he said, 'a Catholic Church spread throughout the world in which no man may err; without the which unity of the Church no man can be saved; but I know perfectly by God's Word that this Church is in all the world and hath not its foundation in Rome only. I acknowledge authority to be given to the spiritualty in matters of religion. I do not deny that in the Sacrament by spirit and grace is the very body and blood of Christ, because that every man by receiving bodily that bread and wine spiritually receiveth the body and blood of Christ, and is made partaker thereby of the merits of Christ's passion.' After their condemnation and degradation the two Bishops were not allowed to remain in peace. Friar Soto, the Spanish Divinity Professor, would needs try his eloquence upon them. He writes, however, to record his disappointment. Latimer would not speak to him at all. Ridley spoke indeed, but he could make no impression upon him. Ridley's last act was a touching appeal addressed to the Queen, and impressed also upon the Bishop of Gloucester, in behalf of some poor people to whom he had granted leases, and for some kindness to be shown to his sister and her three fatherless children. When brought to the stake, near to the western end of Balliol College, old Latimer, with cheery and jocund manner, more as if preparing for some festal banquet than for the agonies of the fire, bade Ridley be of good cheer, for that 'they should that day light such a candle in England as would never be put out.' Ridley too was cheerful and even jubilant. After the needless torture of listening to one of the 'good sermons,' on which the Queen so much insisted, preached by the renegade Doctor Smith, the pyres at length were lighted. Latimer's sufferings were marvellously short. Ridley, like Hooper, endured infinite pain from the clumsiness or brutality with which the fagots had been arranged; but at length all was over.

The next victim was to be one still more illustrious, who, as if to compensate for the many vacillations of his career, was to have a final bitterness added to his death by a vacillation such as was exhibited by none of the less conspicuous martyrs. Archbishop Cranmer had to wait in his prison until his sentence should be received from Rome. This, of course, decreed his degradation, excommunication, and handing over to the secular arm. During this interval Cranmer was beset with continual attacks from the Spaniards who had established themselves at Oxford. The Queen's heart was set on obtaining in his case a peculiar vengeance. He was to be led to deny his convictions from hope of life, and then in spite of his denial to suffer death—to be held up thus to utter scorn and contempt, condemning himself and condemned of others. If the Spanish friars could accomplish this they might hope for the highest favour. Carranza was now Confessor to the Queen, and Carranza's biographer claims for him the credit of having managed everything connected with the execution of Cranmer. Carranza worked upon Cranmer by means of his two friends in Oxford—Soto and Villagarcia. When Ridley and Latimer passed the Arch-

Archbishop Cranmer

bishop's prison on their way to execution, and had hoped to have taken a final farewell of him, they did not see him, because he was then engaged in a dispute with Soto.

But there was something more than disputation going on. There were promises, or at any rate hopes, held out of pardon and favour if the Arch-bishop would recant; and Cranmer, whose character was weak and pliant, yielded to the temptations. Again and again, under pretence of the need of greater distinctness or for some other cause, he was induced to sign recantations no less than six times; and so jubilant were his enemies, that Bonner was actually rash enough to publish a pamphlet containing them before Cranmer's execution. This false step the astute Spaniards endeavoured at once to rectify. They foresaw that the publication of his recantations would be the most likely way to cause the Archbishop to retract them all. Nevertheless some copies of the pamphlet got abroad and even now remain. The series of recantations contained in it show the infinite skill with which the Archbishop was handled. The first three are merely submissions to authority, such as he might have made without any change of sentiments. The fourth is a declaration of adherence to the Catholic faith, such as he himself had voluntarily made at his degradation. Had his assailants been unable to obtain no more, doubtless these would have been used afterwards to discredit the Archbishop. But encouraged by the facility with which they obtained his signature to these, they proceeded to attempt more. The fifth paper is in Latin, and is a most specific and complete retractation, anathematising Luther and Zwingli, acknowledging one only Church of which the Pope is head, the vicar of Christ, to whom all the faithful must submit themselves; admitting transubstantiation, seven sacraments and purgatory, the wholesome custom of praying to saints, and an agreement in all things with the Catholic and Roman Church's belief. The sixth paper is of a similar character, being also in Latin. It is conjectured that it was written by Cardinal Pole, who probably thought he could improve on what had been already signed; there is, however, no proof that Cranmer ever signed this paper. The seventh is Cranmer's own composition, being his prayer and dying speech, but *not as he delivered it*. The Archbishop had, without question, been overcome to sign, through hope of life, that which his conscience did not approve.

But when the end really came, there came a return of fortitude and a better mind. On March 21 (1556), the Archbishop was led to St. Mary's Church, being under the impression (as seems most probable) that after his public recantation his life would be spared. He had, however, resolved that he would not purchase deliverance at such a price, and after a devout prayer and the deepest expressions of contrition, he continued, 'Now I come to the great thing that so much troubleth my conscience, more than anything that ever I did or said in my whole life, and that is the setting abroad of a writing contrary to the truth, which now here I renounce and refuse as things written with my hand contrary to the truth which I thought in my heart, and were written for fear of death, and to save my

Retracts his recantations

life if it might be; and that is all such bills and papers which I have written or signed with my hand since my degradation, wherein I have written many things untrue. And forasmuch as my hand offended, writing contrary to my heart, my hand shall first be punished therefore; for may I come to the fire it shall first be burned. And as for the Pope, I refuse him as Christ's enemy and Anti-Christ, with all his false doctrine. And as for the Sacrament, I believe as I have taught against the Bishop of Winchester.' At this bold declaration a general hubbub was raised in the audience, who had expected something quite different. Dr. Cole, the preacher, called aloud that the heretic's mouth should be stopped, and he was quickly dragged away to the stake.

The Spanish friars, wofully disappointed, now renewed their attacks, threatening him with the pains of hell if he did not instantly change his tone. But Cranmer disregarded them, and endowed at the last with a constancy which he had never known before, thrust his right hand into the flame and held it steadily there till it was consumed. His death soon followed, apparently without much suffering.

His execution

For more than twenty years the Archbishop had been the chief mover of reformation in the English Church, and though he had committed many faults, he had also been the cause of a vast amount of good. In the time of Henry VIII., too subservient to the King's imperious will; in the time of Edward, too forward to act without waiting for the due and deliberate consent of the Church; Erastian in his views on Church government, unstable in his theology,

His character

he cannot be placed among our greatest prelates or divines. But he was mild, tolerant, moderate and fair; an earnest seeker for truth; with a burning zeal to benefit others, and a sincere spirit of devotion; not a resolute nor clear-sighted man, he was still in his generation a great benefactor to his Church and country.

Archbishop Cranmer seems almost a solitary instance among the persecuted Reformers of a temporary yielding through fear of death. In looking over the records of their sufferings, and reading their confessions of faith, many of which are preserved in Strype and Foxe, we are amazed at the calm constancy of their courage, and the simple, earnest, and scriptural tone of their declarations of faith, entirely in accordance with the Articles and Prayer-books set forth in King Edward's days.

<small>Constancy of the Reformers</small>

In December, 1555, was brought to the stake a very distinguished scholar and divine, of the particulars of whose condemnation very minute details, written by himself, remain to us. This was John Philpot, Archdeacon of Winchester, formerly a Fellow of New College, Oxford. Philpot had been one of the five divines who, in the first Convocation of Queen Mary, had boldly undertaken to dispute against the Romish doctrine of the mass, and this had never been forgiven him. He was a man of singular power and readiness in disputation, and as the Romish divines had been unable to contend with him in argument, they had, with great unfairness (inasmuch as all discussions in Convocation were held to be privileged), induced his ordinary to commit him to prison on the charge of heresy. Here he might probably have remained long

<small>Archdeacon Philpot</small>

enough, inasmuch as Gardiner was in no mood to continue these trials for heresy; but the Queen's order to justices of the peace to search out heretics and bring them to their ordinaries touched him. Philpot was brought from his prison before a party of magistrates, and having been treated very rudely by them was sent to Lollards Tower to be judged by the Bishop of London. At this Bonner was by no means pleased. He did not wish to be constituted the ordinary of Philpot, who belonged to the diocese of Winchester. But it was said that the heresy was spoken in the diocese of London, and he must judge the matter. Philpot was accordingly confined in the coal-house of the Bishop of London's palace, and from time to time was brought before the Bishop, who was sometimes aided by one party of assistants, sometimes by another. He constantly refused Bonner's jurisdiction, and claimed privilege for what he had said in the Convocation House; but at length, articles being objected to him, he was compelled to answer, and was condemned for heresy. The records of the thirteen examinations which Philpot underwent, and which are left us by his own hand, as they do credit to his acuteness and knowledge of law and divinity, so also testify to the evident desire of the Bishops to save him, if possible, from the heretic's doom. Bonner, though rough and sometimes brutal, was not unkind to him upon the whole. Some of the other prelates besought him with most friendly sympathy to enable them to obtain his release. Philpot, however, would not yield, and there was a stern power behind the bishops which would not admit of any compromise. Bonner says, with evident annoyance at the part he was obliged to play, 'I marvel that other men will trouble me with their matters, but I must be obedient to my betters, and I wis men speak otherwise of me than I deserve.' Heath, Tonstal, Day, and the other prelates who examined Philpot, felt doubtless that the burning of so distinguished a man would be a scandal before Christendom; but burned he was, notwithstanding.

The Bishops were being driven on in spite of themselves. All, we may believe, were unwilling to act in *The Bishops driven on unwillingly* the persecution. Many, in spite of the impulse which they received, never acted, and there were many dioceses free from burnings. A Commission was issued, February 8, 1557, to two bishops (Bonner and Thirlby), Dr. Cole, Dean of St. Paul's, and about twenty laymen, in which the question of sedition and disaffection was skilfully mixed up with that of heresy. The Commissioners, or any three of them, had the fullest and most arbitrary powers given to them to fine, imprison, *or otherwise punish*. Heretics were to be remitted to their ordinaries if they persisted in their heresy, but all persons refusing to hear mass or to go in procession might be summarily dealt with. This Commission caused the greatest consternation, as it was thought to be the beginning of the Inquisition, and a machinery for superseding the ordinary laws.

Nor was it only the Bishops who shrank from the odious tasks forced upon them. The sheriffs, to whom *Lay officers shrink from acting* the execution of the sentence belonged, also exhibited reluctance to carry it out. Complaints were brought in 1557 to the Council, of the sheriffs of Kent, Essex, Suffolk, and Staffordshire, of the Mayor of Rochester and the Bailiff of Colchester, that they had delayed proceeding to the execution of those who had been handed over to them by the ordinary. They were reprimanded, and ordered to proceed at once. The Council-book also contains a letter (August 1, 1558) reproving the sheriff of Hampshire for staying the execution of a man who offered to recant.

The vengeance would thus seem to have increased in intensity and bitterness as it went on. The most fiendish act of all was, perhaps, the publishing of a proclamation that no one should presume to pray for the sufferers, or should say 'God help them!' on pain of severe punishment. Neither age, sex, nor condition sufficed to shield. Five bishops, twenty-one divines, eight gentlemen of position, and about 250 of the tradesman and husbandman class, of whom about forty were women, are believed, after careful investigations, to represent the number of sufferers.[1] About sixty died in prison. The nobility were mostly ready to accept the Romish faith. Only one, the second Earl of Bedford, appears to have suffered imprisonment. 'The same accommodating spirit,' says

Number of the sufferers

[1] Heylin's summary is:—

Bishops	5
Clergy	21
Gentlemen	8
Artificers	84
Husbandmen and servants	100
Wives	26
Widows	20
Virgins	9
Boys	2
Infants	2
	277

Hallam, 'characterised upon the whole the clergy, and would have been far more general if a considerable number had not availed themselves of the permission to marry.' The taking advantage of this permission furnishes some clue (not a complete or satisfactory one) to the number of clergy who had embraced the tenets of the Reformation. Burnet computes the married clergy at 3,000; Lingard at 1,500.

It is certain, however, that many who were indifferent or opposed to reforming tenets at the accession of Mary became hearty favourers of them before her miserable reign was ended. 'The strongest proof of this,' says Hallam, 'may be drawn from the acquiescence of the great body of the kingdom in the re-establishment of Protestantism by Elizabeth, when compared with the seditions and discontent on that account under Edward.' The fires of Smithfield, the cruelties of the Spaniard, and the miserable decadence of the kingdom, had made the name of Rome more hateful in England than it had ever been, and made reaction impossible. The traditional jealousy of France was now eclipsed and obscured by that bitter detestation of the Spaniard, which for many generations was the most prominent feeling in the English mind. Hasty and unjust measures, feeble and vacillating counsels, the dread of fanaticism, the love for old customs, checked men's acceptance of the Reformation under Edward, and the attempt to press it on too violently threatened the most serious danger. But in the midst of the scenes of blood and misery which were enacted before the eyes of Englishmen and Englishwomen during Mary's reign, all this was forgotten, and

Reformation advanced by the persecution

the weaknesses and difficulties of the last reign seemed to be virtues and glories compared with the wretchedness of the present.

To those of the clergy who were ready to submit to the yoke of Rome, the Queen was kind and liberal. *The Queen's benefactions* She would gladly have seen all the abbey and church lands restored to their former owners, but to this her subjects were by no means ready to consent. She refounded the Abbey of Westminster and many other monastic houses. She surrendered to the Church the first fruits and tenths which had been grasped by King Henry VIII.[1] The Cardinal Archbishop also showed himself a vigorous and skilful administrator.

But the curse of blood was upon everything. The Queen, childless, isolated, neglected by her husband, *Misery of the period* whom she fondly loved, in constant fear of plots and conspiracies, dreading her subjects and dreaded by them, was the most miserable woman in the land. Cardinal Pole, who had done so much for Rome, was denounced to the Inquisition, condemned by the Pope, superseded in his office of Legate. In the bitterness which took possession of him, he is said to have entered at last zealously into the persecution from which he had shrunk at first. The month of November (1558) brought a happy relief to the persecuted Church of England. The Queen died on the 17th and Cardinal Pole the following day. Only one week before her death five persons were burned at Canterbury, where the suffragan bishop Thornden, and the archdeacon

---

[1] Heylin says: 'She lost nothing by the bargain, the clergy paid her back again in their bills of subsidies.'—*Eccl. Rest* 83.

Harpsfield, had distinguished themselves as persecutors throughout. But in the cathedral city of the Cardinal's diocese these victims must have been sacrificed by his special authorisation. Heylin says, 'It had been prayed or prophesied by those five martyrs, when they were at the stake, that they might be the last who should suffer death in that manner, and by God's mercy so it proved, they being the last which suffered death under the severity of this persecution.'

CHAPTER XIV.

THE ENGLISH REFORMERS ABROAD.

1553-1558.

It is not to be supposed that the persecution of the English Reformers, though prosecuted with the utmost cruelty, availed to destroy or drive away all those who openly professed these opinions in England. There is evidence that even in the most dangerous spot in the country, in Bonner's own diocese, there existed a congregation, varying in number from forty up to two hundred, which maintained constant meetings for religion in London during the whole of Mary's reign. The ministers of this congregation were Scambler, afterwards Bishop of Peterborough; Foule, Rough, who was put to death by Bonner; Augustine Bernher, and finally Thomas Bentham, who continued in the charge till the death of Queen Mary. And if this was the case in London,

Reformed congregations in England

doubtless in many parts of the country, where there was comparatively no danger, congregations of those who held to the form of religion legalised under King Edward would be found. In England the bond of a common danger would avail to hold together those who were bitterly opposed to the Roman and Spanish religion, however much they might differ among themselves. But that very great differences did exist among them cannot be doubted. There were those who held loyally to the English Prayer-book; there were 'gospellers' who would have everything levelled down to the platform of Calvin and Zwingli; there were Anabaptists, the enemies of all restraints, and of all kinds of ministry whether Episcopal or Presbyterian. These differences among the Reformers, concealed in England by the circumstances of their position, when these circumstances were absent came out strongly, and produced disastrous effects.

It is conjectured that about eight hundred persons known to be of strong reforming views escaped from England at the beginning of the reign of Mary, and found asylums in Switzerland and the free cities on the Rhine. The Lutheran cities of Germany, being more under the dread of the Emperor, do not seem to have done much in the way of hospitality to the fugitives; but the French and Swiss Reformers were most kind and sympathetic. Five bishops escaped—Poynet, Barlow, Scory, Coverdale, Bale of Ossory; five deans—Cox, Horne, Haddon, Turner, Sampson; three archdeacons—Cranmer, Aylmer, Bullingham. Among the better known divines were Grindal, King, Sandys, Jewel, Reynolds,

The Reformers who escaped

Pilkington, Nowel, Knox, Gilby, Whittingham, Foxe. There were also the Duchess of Suffolk, and her second husband, Mr. Bertie; Sir Richard Morrison, Sir Anthony Cook, and Sir John Cheke. The fugitives distributed themselves in some seven or eight cities where reforming opinions were safe from persecution, but the greatest numbers seem to have been brought together at Zürich and at Frankfort. Those who first arrived at Frankfort were kindly greeted by the colony of French Protestants established there; and through their support obtained leave from the civic authorities both to remain in the city, and to practise their religious worship in the church used by the French, at the times when the latter did not need it. Only a condition was laid down, viz., 'That they should not dissent from the Frenchmen in doctrine or ceremonies, and that they should approve and subscribe the same confession of faith that the Frenchmen had then presented, and were about to put in print.'

The English exiles took counsel as to what sort of a service they should use, and came to the conclusion to use the English service in part, but without responses or the Litany, and without surplice; to sing 'a Psalm in metre to a plain tune'; the minister to use an extemporary prayer, and 'so to proceed to the sermon'; after the sermon another extemporary prayer 'for all estates, and for our country of England'; then the Lord's Prayer and the rehearsal of the Articles of Belief, then another Psalm and the Blessing. This service may have been very edifying; but it was not the service of the Church of England as settled in the Prayer-book, and it could

The English service at Frankfort

The English Reformers Abroad

hardly fail to be displeasing to those who were zealous for the preservation of the work done by the Church in the days of King Edward. 'As touching the ministration of the Sacraments, sundry things were also by common consent omitted, as superfluous and superstitious.' A minister 'and deacons' were chosen, and in fact a complete Presbyterian settlement was effected.

Then the Frankfort men, being greatly pleased with their work, invited the exiles from other quarters to repair to this favoured place. In answer to this letter a reply came from the English at Strasburg, recommending the Frankfort men to put themselves under the direction of one of the exiled bishops, such as Bishop Scory. This greatly annoyed the Frankfort body, who did not want a bishop, but had already written to Knox at Geneva, Haddon at Strasburg, and Lever at Zürich, requesting them to take charge of the church in Presbyterian fashion.

Others invited to Frankfort

Next came a reply from Zürich stating that the fugitives there were well established, and had no desire to move; but if their brethren at Frankfort thought it absolutely necessary for the preservation of the faith that they should join them, they would do so. This, however, must be on the condition that 'the order last taken in the Church of England should be adhered to;' for, say they, 'we are fully determined to admit and use no other.' The Zürich party also sent one of their number, Chambers, to arrange for the junction of the two bodies if he found all things suitable for it. But when Chambers came to Frankfort, he found that the

Stipulation for use of the English Prayer-book

English there were not at all prepared to guarantee 'the full use of the English book,' and the negotiation came to an end.

In the meantime the Frankforters had, by an unanimous vote, invited John Knox, from Geneva, to be their minister. Knox, a Scotchman by birth, had lived for some time in England, in considerable repute as one of King Edward's chaplains, and one of the royal itinerant preachers. He had, however, no love for the settlement of the English Church or its services, as his conduct at Frankfort soon showed.

John Knox

Before his arrival the Frankfort body had answered the Zürich men, giving a very modified approval of the English Prayer-book, condemning some of the ceremonies, and saying that doubtless much more would have been changed had not the Reformation been suddenly checked. The Churchmen at Zürich, alarmed at this serious manifestation of dissent, sent back Chambers, and with him Grindal, to endeavour to persuade the Frankfort body to stand loyally by the English Prayer-book, on the ground that dissent from it in any way would cast a slur on the English Reformation and on those who were suffering for it at home. The answer of Knox and Whittingham was, that they were willing to accept the book so far as it was grounded on the Word of God— the interpretation to be put on the Word of God being, of course, their own. Upon this the negotiations were broken off; and the Frankfort congregation asked Knox to administer the Holy Communion according to 'the order of Geneva.' Knox hesitated to do this, 'thinking,' says Heylin, 'himself as able to make a rule as

Dispute as to the English Prayer-book

any Calvin of them all,' neither would he use the English book, to which he strongly objected.

Lever had now joined him in the pastorate, and they came to the resolution to submit the matter to Calvin at Geneva, sending him the Prayer-book in Latin translation, and giving him a description or comment upon the book 'to which some of their countrymen went about to force them, and would admit no other.' They requested his solution of the difficulty. Calvin was well enough acquainted with the English Prayer-book before this, and did not gain much new information from the description now sent to him, which is an unfair and clumsy document. He replied, in a contemptuous manner, that the English book contained many 'tolerable fooleries,' but he would not have them 'fierce over those whose infirmity will not suffer them to ascend an higher step.' The effect of this letter was to cause the adoption at Frankfort of an order for the Holy Communion, 'some part taken forth of the English book and other things put to.'

Calvin's opinion of the Prayer-book

At this juncture Cox, late Dean of Christ Church and Westminster, and one of the compilers of the English Prayer-book, arrived at Frankfort, accompanied by a large party of English Churchmen. Cox insisted on saying aloud the responses as in the English Prayer-book, and one of his party even read the Litany in the church. Upon this he was vehemently attacked by Knox, and the original body of fugitives appealed to the magistrates.

Dr. Cox

As a counter-move the new-comers represented to the magistrates that Knox, in a book which he had published, had described the Emperor Charles as Nero.

Upon this the magistrates immediately took alarm, and Knox was ordered to leave the city. Cox had also contrived to get on his side a nephew of the chief magistrate of Frankfort, and by his influence it was directed that the English Prayer-book should henceforth be used in the Frankfort congregation. This arrangement being very distasteful to some, a secession of the malcontents under Whittingham and Foxe was made to Basle and Geneva. The congregation at Frankfort remained under the ministry of Whitehead and Horne, assisted by Mullings and Treherne; but did not, alas, remain in peace. These dissensions are a very uninviting subject; but the consideration of them is necessary to the understanding of the Reformation movement, as all the controversies which afterwards troubled the Church of England were now hatched.

Knox banished

The first dispute had been on the matter of the ceremonies. The second, which is now to be touched, was on the question of discipline. Already Knox and Goodman, at Geneva, had completely rejected the 'whole frame and fashion of the Reformation made in England, and had conformed themselves wholly to the fashions of the Church of Geneva.' The same spirit was now exhibited at Frankfort. A dispute had arisen between Horne, the pastor (Whitehead having now gone), and one Ashley, a lay member of the congregation. Horne, supported by Chambers and some others, endeavoured to rule matters with a high hand. Ashley's party held meetings to resist their authority. Presently they drew up a 'book of discipline,' in which 'the supreme power in

New dissensions on discipline

all ecclesiastical causes was put into the hands of the congregations, and the disposal of the public monies committed to the trust of certain officers by the name of deacons.' The dispute becoming more serious, the interference of the magistrates was invoked, who referred the settlement of the matter to Cox, Sandys, and Bertie.

The settlement proposed by the referees did not suit the discipline party, who refused to abandon their scheme. In consequence Horne and Chambers resigned their offices, and retired to Strasburg, leaving the congregation at Frankfort to be worked on the Presbyterian platform. 'Hence,' says Heylin, 'the beginning of the Puritan faction against the rites and ceremonies of the Church; that of the Presbyterians against the bishops or episcopal government; and finally, that also of the Independents against the superintendency of pastors and elders.'

The Frankfort congregation becomes Presbyterian

The other English colonies do not seem to have been distracted with the same troubles that befell the congregation at Frankfort. At Embden, Bishop Scory presided over a congregation in quiet. The Duchess of Suffolk and her husband had settled at Wesel; but afterwards, at the invitation of the Palsgrave, they removed to the neighbourhood of Heidelberg. The Wesel congregation then migrated to Basle. Lever obtained permission from the authorities of Bern to open a church in their territories, and he chose Aarau, where the 'congregation lived together in godly quietness among themselves with great favour of the people.'

The other English settlements

At the death of Queen Mary an attempt appears to have been made by the party at Geneva to bring about a sort of united action among the various congregations, on the ground of not 'contending for superfluous ceremonies and other like trifles.' Keith was dispatched by them to endeavour to effect this. The answer which came from Frankfort shows that a complete change had by this time been effected in the state of things there. Only four of those who were engaged in the original disputes remained. The present members of the congregation replied to Geneva in a very sensible strain. 'We purpose to submit ourselves to such orders as shall be established by authority, being not of themselves wicked; so we would wish you willingly to do the same. For whereas all the reformed churches differ among themselves in divers ceremonies, and yet agree in the unity of doctrine, we see no inconvenience if we use some ceremonies diverse from them, so that we agree in the chief points of our religion.'

Action of the Geneva body

The calm spirit which appears in these words was not, however, shared by the majority of the English fugitives who hastened back at the death of the persecuting Queen. Most of them undoubtedly were possessed with the notion of a 'further reformation.' They did not anticipate merely the revival of the old book, and even an increase in ceremonial and strictness. Having become accustomed to the freer ways and more democratic life of the communities where they had long sojourned, they did not contemplate with satisfaction being regulated by autocratic bishops, and kept to a hard and fast uniformity.

Spirit of the reformers who returned

Some of them preferred on principle the Genevan platform, or the government of the Church by an oligarchy. Many more, without distinctly adopting this, desired freedom; that ceremonies should be left as matters indifferent, and that each man should be allowed to treat the rule according to his conscience. The first of these became the parents of the Separatists, the second of the Unconformable or Nonconformist clergy, of whom we hear so much in the days of Elizabeth. Thus as the Marian persecution had endeared the Church to the people, and strengthened it in the affections of many, so the sojourn of the exiles abroad had sowed the seed of contentiousness, Precisianism, and Puritanism, from which the Church was afterwards so terribly to suffer.

CHAPTER XV.

THE RECOVERY OF THE CHURCH OF ENGLAND.

1558-1559.

IT was assumed as certain by the reforming party that Queen Elizabeth, who had been in peril of her life from her sister, and had been subjected to constraint and ill-usage for her inclination towards the Reformation, would, on her accession, take a decided line against the old superstitions. At once, therefore, in many places the people began to pull down images and to pour contempt upon the priests and their service. Under Mary's tyranny the nation, which had slowly and reluctantly accepted

Queen Elizabeth's religious policy

the changes made under King Edward, had become fiercely Protestant. But Queen Elizabeth had no intention of compromising her position, and endangering her throne by any violent partisan action. The powers of Europe were hostile to her; a large section of her own subjects would be ready to join them against one who would certainly be excommunicated and declared illegitimate by the Pope. There was need of the most consummate prudence if the State was to be saved from danger, and the Church reinstated in its national position. This gift of prudence and policy Elizabeth happily possessed in a remarkable degree. 'This Queen,' says Burnet, 'had a strange art of insinuating herself into the affections of her people.' She was determined to carry, if possible, all parties with her. Thus, when she went to her coronation she clasped the Bible to her bosom with such fervour that she drew tears from many of the spectators; but the ceremony of her coronation was performed, not by one of the reforming bishops, but by Oglethorpe, Bishop of Carlisle, with all the old ceremonies. Again, she did not at once sanction the use of the English Prayer-book, which was not as yet legal, but adopted a modified form of worship such as had been used in King Henry's days, and by a Proclamation enjoined this upon the people.

This document ran as follows: 'The Queen's Majesty understanding that there be certain persons

Proclamation about preaching

having in times past the office of ministry in the Church, which now do purpose to use their former office in preaching and ministry, and partly have attempted the same, assembling specially in the city of London, in sundry places, great number of people; whereupon riseth among the common sort not only unfruitful disputes in matters of religion, but also contention and occasion to break common quiet; hath therefore according to the authority committed to her Highness, for the quiet governance of all manner of her subjects, thought it necessary to charge and command, like as hereby her Highness doth charge and command, all manner of her subjects, as well those as be called to the ministry in the Church as all others; that they do forbear to preach or teach, or to give audience to any manner of doctrine or preaching, other than to the Gospels and Epistles commonly called the Gospel and Epistle of the day, and to the Ten Commandments in the vulgar tongue, without exposition or addition of any manner sense or meaning to be applied and added; or to use any manner of public prayer, rite or ceremony in the Church, but that which is already used and by law received, as the Common Litany used at this present in Her Majesty's Chapel, and the Lord's Prayer and the Creed in English; until consultation may be had by Parliament by Her Majesty, and her three estates of this realm, for the better conciliation and accord of such causes as at this present are moved in matters and ceremonies of religion.' This was to bring back the state of things to what it was in King Henry's time, and could not have satisfied the more ardent reformers. The Latin mass was still to be said with the English parts which had been then introduced.

In a paper of recommendations offered to Secretary Cecil, it is suggested that there be no further alterations 'except it be to receive the Communion as her Majesty pleaseth, at high feasts; and that where there be more chaplains at the mass, that they do always communicate with the executor in both kinds. And for her Highness' conscience, till then, if there be some other devout sort of prayer or memory said, and the seldomer, mass.' This advice is somewhat enigmatical, but it clearly contemplates the Queen continuing to be present at mass according to the old form. The only alteration which she required the officiating priest to make was, the disuse of the elevation of the consecrated elements.

The recommendations given to Cecil

And it is probable that this form of service would have quite satisfied the Queen for a continuance. 'The Queen,' says Burnet, ' had been bred up from her infancy with a hatred of the Papacy and a love for the Reformation; but yet, as her first impressions in her father's reign were in favour of such old rites as he had still retained, so in her own nature she loved state and some magnificence in religion as in everything else. She thought that in her brother's reign they had stripped it too much of external ornaments, and made their doctrine too narrow in some points. She inclined to keep up images in churches, and to have the manner of Christ's presence in the Sacrament left in some general words, that those who believed the corporal presence might not be driven away from the Church by too nice an explanation of it.' But though it is possible that a very moderate amount of reformation might have satisfied the Queen, she knew well that nothing less would satisfy the great body of her subjects than that the Church of England should be ' reduced to its former purity '; and the question at once arose how this was to be done.

Elizabeth's own religious views

The Convocation was bitterly hostile to reforming views. Under Mary, all the clergy in high places who had been favourers of the Reformation had been assiduously weeded out. The revival of the illegality of clerical marriage had served to oust the greater part of those incumbents who were of similar views. Many of the livings had fallen to dispossessed monks and friars, so that the proctors elected for the clergy would assuredly be no favourers of the Reformation. The bishops, deans and archdeacons, who form the majority of Convocation, would be still less likely to be so. From this clerical body, therefore, which would assemble with the Parliament, nothing in the way of bringing back the settlement made under King Edward could be hoped for. The Parliament might be more easily handled and better trusted; but to establish a form of religious service simply by the action of Parliament, in opposition to the voice of the spiritualty, was a dangerous measure, and more even than had been attempted in the rash days of King Edward. In the State Paper already quoted, a cautious course is recommended. The bishops and dignified clergy 'being in manner all made and chosen such as were thought the stoutest and mightiest champions of the Pope's church,' and having enriched themselves illegally in Queen Mary's time, were to be reduced to order by the Præmunire statute, and made to abjure the Pope of Rome, and to conform themselves to the new alteration. In place of the Convocation, a Committee of Divines was to be appointed to review the Service-books of King Edward, and to specify what, if any, alterations should be made, before one of them,

The question of the bringing back the reformed settlement

either the first form or the second, should be re-established by Act of Parliament. Both of these books had the sanction of Convocation, and had been prepared solely by divines. To fall back simply on the constitutional arrangement of the former reign, which was a natural sequence from the acts of the State and Church under Henry VIII., and to disregard the violent interruption and un-English doings of Mary, was clearly the best policy and a proceeding justifiable on all grounds. Thus the reforming party would have all that they could fairly claim, while a door might be opened for those who favoured Romish views, by introducing some alterations in the Communion Office, which had been hardly treated in the second book of King Edward. The persons recommended for the important task of reviewing the Service-book were Bill, Parker, May, Cox, Whitehead, Grindal, and Pilkington. They were to be called together and assisted by Sir Thomas Smith, and when they had come to a decision 'to draw in other men of learning, and grave and apt men,' to confirm their views.

These persons in effect were appointed for this work, with the addition of Sandys; and when Parker could not act on account of illness, Guest was put in his place. The work was immediately commenced, and was done with great secrecy, the Queen being very careful that nothing decisive should be known as to her intentions in matters of religion until Parliament met. What the temper of that body would be as regards changes in religion was of course very doubtful. In the House of Lords the whole of the bishops, and many of the other peers, would certainly oppose any

The Commission to review the Prayer-book

The Recovery of the Church of England 157

reforming movement. The Crown had great power in influencing elections for the Commons; but it was not probable that it would be able to bring together a House altogether prepared to reject the religious settlement so lately voted and established. Meantime, in the preparation of the Prayer-book to be submitted to Parliament, the same opposing forces were at work as had been observable in the time of King Edward. There was the love of antiquity and the old ceremonial face to face with the eager desire to make much greater changes than had been already made, and to advance in the direction of the foreign reformers. The Queen was the upholder of the first view, and Sir William Cecil endeavoured to impress the Queen's opinion upon the revisers, who themselves were mostly in favour of a more drastic reformation. Many of them had lived abroad and had become intimate with the foreign reformers. Some of the body were certainly disposed to go great lengths in change. Parker, the most moderate of them, was absent through illness. There was an evident danger of strong measures being applied to the Service-book, which would hopelessly alienate the moderate Romanists whom it was the Queen's policy to conciliate.

Then Sir W. Cecil came to the rescue, handing to the revisers a paper of questions which clearly indi-*Sir W. Cecil's questions* cated the Queen's wishes, and which, if it were not accepted altogether, would certainly serve to modify their desire for violent change. This paper puts in a plea for the ceremonies of King Edward's first book. It suggests that the crucifix should be retained. To this we know the Queen was quite determined to adhere as regards her own chapel. That the cope should be used at the celebration of the Holy Communion; that processions should be used; prayer for the dead, and the prayers taken out of the first Communion Office be restored. What was going on soon came to be known among the leading reforming divines. Thus Jewel writes to Peter Martyr: 'The scenic apparatus of divine worship is now under agitation; and these very things which you and I have so often laughed at are now seriously and solemnly maintained by certain persons (for we are not consulted), as if the Christian religion could not exist without something tawdry. Our minds indeed are not sufficiently disengaged to make these fooleries of much importance. Others are seeking after a golden, or as it seems to me, a leaden mediocrity, and are crying out that the half is better than the whole.' The revisers, however, were not prepared to accept the suggestions which came to them through Sir W. Cecil from the Queen. Dr. Guest drew up an answer to them all, in what may be called the Protestant sense. The revisers held to the second book of King Edward rather than to the first, and as far as can be ascertained (for the subject is involved in obscurity), the book left their hands with only three alterations, viz. an addition of certain lessons to be used on Sundays; an amended form of the Litany; the bringing back of the words to be used to communicants of the first book in union with those of the second. These, it seems, were intended by the revisers to be the only alterations made in the second book of King Edward when it was presented to Parliament.

But it will presently appear that the opposing influence which they had set aside in their review was not to be so easily disposed of. The Act of Parliament (Act of Uniformity) was actually drawn, enacting the establishment of the book with these three alterations specified, 'and none other or otherwise,' but at the close of this very Act occurs a clause which, in fact, did legalise another and a very important alteration. 'Provided always, and be it enacted, that such ornaments of the Church and of the ministers thereof shall be retained, and be used, as was in this Church of England by authority of Parliament in the second year of King Edward VI., until other order shall be therein taken by the authority of the Queen's Majesty, with the advice of her Commissioners appointed and authorised under the Great Seal of England for causes ecclesiastical, or of the Metropolitan of this realm.' This proviso involved the abrogation of at least one, if not both, of the first Rubricks in King Edward's book. How did it get into an Act of Parliament which in its previous clauses expressly excludes it? Evidently it must have been added to the Act by the direction of the Queen herself, when the draft was considered in Council; and being drawn in a provisional form, it was perhaps held that it might fairly be defended as not making any actual alteration in the previous wording of the Act.[1] More will have to

[1] Strype is of opinion that the book as it came from the revisers allowed the communicants to receive standing or kneeling (according to Guest's paper), and that the words 'standing or' were struck out in Parliament. This may have been the case, for as Edward's book has simply kneeling, this would not require specifying as a change.

be presently said as to the Elizabethan Prayer-book; but first it is necessary to consider the circumstances connected with the passing of the Act of Parliament which authorised it.

Parliament met on January 25 (1559). It was opened by a speech from the Lord Keeper which was intended to be a manifesto. He said that 'the Queen had God before her eyes and was not unmindful of precepts and divine counsels; that she required them, for the duty they bore to God and their service to her and their country, that they would with all humbleness, singleness and pureness of mind, use their whole endeavour and diligence to establish that which by their wisdoms should be thought most meet for the well preserving of this godly purpose, and that without respect of honour, rule or sovereignty, profit, pleasure or ease; or of anything that might touch any person in estimation or opinion, of wit, learning or knowledge; and without regard of other affection; that in their conference about this they would wholly forbear as a great enemy to good counsel, all manner of contention, reasonings, disputes; that no contentious or contumelious words as *heretic, schismatic, papist*, should be used. And that as nothing should be advised or done that might in any way breed or nourish any kind of idolatry or superstition, so heed was to be taken that by licentious or loose handling any occasion might be given whereby contempt or irreverent behaviour towards God and godly things might creep in.' The Parliament fully responded to this appeal. It showed itself, indeed, somewhat too ready to help the Queen at the expense of the Church, rather than out of the pockets of the laity, giving her the first-fruits and tenths which Mary had restored to the Church, and again legalising the evil practice of exchange by the Crown of impropriate tithes for manors at the vacancy of a bishopric. It also readily recognised the Queen's title and legitimacy.

But the Bill for 'Restoring the Supremacy,' which was sent up from the Commons on February 27, encountered considerable difficulty in the House of Lords. This important Bill was, in fact, some two months in its passage through Parliament, additions having been constantly made to it, and considerable changes introduced. The title finally adopted for it was 'An Act for restoring to the Crown the ancient jurisdiction over the State, ecclesiastical and spiritual.' The Act did in effect, though not in name, bring back the dominating power of Henry VIII., and as he was enabled to commit this irresponsible power to a lay Vicar-General, so this Act enabled the Queen to erect a 'High Commission Court,' which should be empowered to 'visit, reform, correct and amend all such errors, heresies, schisms, abuses, offences, contempts and enormities whatsoever, which by any manner, spiritual or ecclesiastical power, authority, or jurisdiction, can or may lawfully be reformed, ordered, redressed, corrected, restrained or amended.' Thus, as Collier observes, 'the whole Church discipline seems transferred upon the Crown'; and, as he points out, no mention being made of the necessity of spiritual persons being appointed on the High Commission Court, the whole of this discipline might be exercised by laymen. For the guidance of such Commissioners,

marginal note: Supremacy Act

who might be presumed not to be learned in ecclesiastical matters, the Act vouchsafes to define what is to be accounted heresy, namely, what had 'heretofore been determined, ordered, or adjudged to be heresy by the authority of the canonical Scriptures, or by the first four General Councils, or any of them, or by any other General Council wherein the same was declared heresy by the express and plain words of the said canonical Scriptures, or such as hereafter shall be judged, ordered, or determined to be heresy by the High Court of Parliament of this realm, with the assent of the clergy in their Convocation.' The Bill was strongly opposed, as might have been expected, by the ten bishops, who were all that were able to be present of the number of those appointed under Queen Mary. Heath, Archbishop of York and Mary's Lord Chancellor, spoke strongly against it. But it was at length carried by a small majority (April 29), containing a proviso that it should be supported by an oath, to be taken by all clergymen and public functionaries, 'to defend all jurisdictions, privileges, pre-eminences and authorities, granted or belonging to the Queen's Highness, her heirs and successors, or united and annexed to the Imperial Crown of this realm.' In this Act the Queen is not styled Supreme Head of the Church, as her father and her sister had been, but Supreme Governor—a more fitting title. The Act also repealed the ecclesiastical legislation made or revived in the past reign, and revived the ecclesiastical acts of Henry and Edward. One Act, however, was not revived; the bishops were not henceforth to be appointed by letters patent, and to use the royal name in their orders, but were to be elected, as of old, by their Chapters, and to use ecclesiastical jurisdiction. The powers thus entrusted to the Crown appear portentous, and in principle are perhaps indefensible. But in the utterly disorganised state of the Church after so many changes, they were greatly needed and were practically valuable. The Queen had no intention of appointing laymen to represent her supremacy, being extremely jealous of lay interference in Church matters. But she wished to arm the bishops with full power and authority, and having thus armed them, she was fully determined that they should do the work of discipline—from which indeed many of them afterwards shrank in a very cowardly manner.

Before this Act had become law, the Act for Uniformity of Public Worship was brought into the Lords (April 25), and after three days' discussion, in which some very able speeches were made against it by the Romanist bishops, was passed by a small majority. It has been already pointed out that the Act contained a proviso which was not in accordance with the description of the Prayer-book as given in the earlier part of it.

The Act of Uniformity

In addition to this, when the Prayer-book appeared in print it contained other alterations not specified by the Act. Very few copies of the Elizabethan Prayer-book remain, but there is none which is in accordance with the description of the book in the Act of Parliament. In the first place, the proviso which had been inserted in the Act appears in the book in the form of two initial Rubricks, which take the place of two similar Rubricks of the book of Edward, from which they altogether differ. Then there are several

The Elizabethan Prayer-book

alterations in the prayers besides what is specified in the Act; and thirdly, the declaration as to kneeling, which appears in the book of Edward, is omitted. This last was probably done on the ground that it was not covered by his Act of Uniformity. That the revisers were somewhat startled by the form which the book ultimately assumed may be inferred from the letter of Dr. Sandys, who, speaking of the Rubricks which legalised the use of the old ecclesiastical vesture, says, 'Our gloss upon this text is, that we shall not be forced to use them, but that others in the meantime shall not convey them away, but that they may remain for the Queen.' It may be questioned, however, whether that was the intention of the Queen, who had no doubt procured the insertion of this Rubrick, the legality of which was covered by the Act of Parliament. That Elizabeth still entertained the desire and hope of introducing more ceremonial and more of the ancient practices into the Church may be inferred from many things, and especially from the history of the Latin Prayerbook, in which the Queen was much interested.

This book, translated by Dr. Walter Haddon at the Queen's desire—the translator taking as his groundwork *The Latin Prayer-Book* Aless's translation of the book of 1549—contains many things which the English Prayerbook does not contain; and it is conjectured with great probability that the Queen's wish in authorising the book by her letters patent (April 1560), was to bring back for the use of the clergy and learned societies the usages of 1549, and so gradually to reintroduce them for the whole Church. In accordance with this, although power was reserved for the Queen in the Act of Uniformity to take further order for ecclesiastical vestments, it is not found that she ever did take such further order, but allowed the vestures of 1549 to remain as the prescribed officiating dress of the clergy, although their use was not enforced. On January 22, 1561, she did indeed publish, under the Great Seal, a 'further order,' but this was merely to legalise the changes in the Calendar of Lessons which had been already prepared; to direct that the decays in churches, and especially in chancels, should be looked to; and that tables of the Ten Commandments should be 'comely set or hung up in the east end of the chancel, to be not only read for edification, but also to give some comely ornament, and demonstration that the same is a place of religion.' It is evident that the desire to make the worship of the Church of England more ceremonious and ornamental was constantly in the Queen's mind.

CHAPTER XVI.

THE BISHOPS AND CLERGY.

THE Parliament had brought back again the reformed Prayer-book of the Church of England, and had overthrown the Romish system established under Queen Mary. But by what agency was the new condition of things to be upheld, and where were to be found the ministers ready to use the English book? Would the incumbents of churches, who had returned gladly to the Romish services under Queen Mary, again abandon them, and

The difficulty of finding clergy for the reformed Church

adopt the English forms, which had been pronounced heretical; and would they go further and recommend the doctrines embodied in them in sermons or homilies? This could hardly be expected. Where also were the bishops to superintend the Church in so critical a juncture, and by judicious discipline to bring about conformity? The supply of fit ministers was the one especial difficulty of the time. Books and laws might be excellent, but without the living agent they would be utterly futile. That this enormous difficulty was got over—that competent bishops were found, and clergy and preachers gradually supplied to the Church at this period—is not the least marvellous fact in the history of the English Reformation. It would of course have been impossible that this should have been done without scandals occurring. That out of the old Marian priests, who in their hearts hated reform, and the fanatical Protestants, driven to fury by the late butcheries, there should at once and easily have been constructed a well-qualified and earnest set of Anglican clergy, who would temperately and wisely work out the system of the English Prayer-book, would have been a greater miracle than could have been expected. No doubt the scandals were many, but order was gradually educed; and long before the end of this eventful reign the Church was well provided with an efficient ministry.

Before however anything is said of the Anglican prelates and clergy, it is necessary to note briefly the fate of those who were in high position at the accession of Elizabeth. Many of the Romish bishops had died just about that time from the quartan fever then very prevalent. Fourteen only were now remaining. These had greatly disobliged the Queen

The Romish bishops and clergy

THE BISHOPS AND CLERGY

by the refusal of all of them (excepting Oglethorpe, of Carlisle), to officiate at her coronation; and by the conduct of some of them in a disputation held at Westminster before the Parliament.

In this the bishops, who had undertaken to conduct the discussion according to certain fixed rules, which had been accepted on their part by Archbishop Heath, afterwards refused to abide by these rules, and broke off the discussion. A very bitter feeling was evoked by this, and two of the Romish bishops, White and Watson, were committed to the Tower. The bishops also strongly opposed both the Supremacy and Uniformity Acts in Parliament, and in Convocation had joined in passing resolutions directly antagonistic to the English Prayer-book. They were in fact, according to their power, carrying on war against the Crown; and if the precedent of the last reign had been followed, would have quickly found themselves in the Tower. But Elizabeth, wiser in her generation, tried conciliatory courses.

The Westminster disputation

On May 15 (1559), all the bishops were called into her presence, and being reminded of the laws lately passed, were invited by her to conform and so retain their Sees. In this request it need not be doubted, from her known sentiments, that the Queen was sincere. But Archbishop Heath thought it his duty to address the Queen on the zeal of her sister Mary for the Church of Rome, and to add the very impolitic suggestion that Mary's acts bound her Majesty and her successors Elizabeth answered with much dignity. 'She owed allegiance to God, but none to the Bishop of Rome; her sister's acts did not bind her, her

The bishops before the Queen

successors or her realms.' The nation had rejected the usurped authority of this bishop, and she for her part absolutely repudiated it, holding her crown only under Christ, and looking upon all those as her enemies who should maintain allegiance to this foreign power.' The bishops retired, somewhat dismayed at the Queen's vigour, and the Council were now convinced that they would have to be treated as enemies. They discovered also, as is said, among the papers left by Queen Mary, a mass of evidence showing the treasonable practices of some of them in King Edward's time.

It was decided, however, not to trouble them on these matters, but simply to propose to them the oath lately enacted in the Supremacy statute. This they all refused to take, and were accordingly deprived. Their after treatment was not specially severe. There were no retaliatory burnings. They suffered a short imprisonment, and then most of them were restored to liberty. Archbishop Heath lived on his own estate at Chobham, and was occasionally visited by the Queen. The amiable Tonstal lived for the short remainder of his life with the new Archbishop of Canterbury, with whom he had much in common. Thirlby, Bishop of Ely, a much inferior man, also 'lived in much ease and credit with the Archbishop for ten years,' when he died. White, a violent man, who with Bishop Watson had threatened to excommunicate the Queen, nevertheless died at liberty. Bourne lived in comfort with Dr. Carew, Dean of Exeter. Turberville and Poole lived in their own houses unmolested. Bayne and Oglethorpe died soon after the beginning of the reign. Watson, 'a sour and morose man,' lived at first in comparative freedom, but after a time, becoming an in-

Their treatment

triguer, was committed to Wisbech Castle, where he died. Scott, Pate, and Goldwell, after some imprisonment, were allowed to go abroad. Bonner, the most obnoxious of all, and who had shown a cruelty and bitterness in persecution with which none of the others are chargeable, lived and died in the Marshalsea. He dared not have ventured out, so infuriated were the people against him; but within the strong walls of the prison 'he lived daintily, having the use of the garden and orchards when he was minded to walk abroad.' The treatment these prelates received was somewhat different from that which Spanish cruelty had accorded to Cranmer, Ridley and Latimer, Hooper and Farrar. Nor was the treatment of the inferior clergy more severe.

The use of the Prayer-book had been appointed under penalties for St. John Baptist's Day (June 24). *The clergy who refused the Prayer-book* But at that time the great majority utterly refused to use it. They were not immediately interfered with. They had seven months for reflection; and they made so good a use of th s interval, that when the Commissioners afterwards made their visitation throughout the whole of the country, a ridiculously small proportion of the clergy then refused to conform. The list, as given in Camden, only amounts to 189;[1] and 'we may reckon,' says that historian, 'in

[1] Bishops	.	.	.	.	.	14
Deans	.	.	.	.	.	12
Archdeacons	.	.	.	.	.	12
Heads of Colleges	.	.	.	.	15
Abbots and Priors	.	.	.	.	6
Prebendaries	.	.	.	.	.	50
Parish priests	.	.	.	.	.	80
						189

Collier's list makes 229.

England above 9,400 ecclesiastical preferments.' It must not, however, be assumed that in all but some one hundred parishes there were incumbents conforming, however unwillingly. A great number doubtless resigned their cures. There was a pressing and immediate demand for clergy.

But in order to provide clergy there must first be bishops, and to this the Queen and her ministers had to turn their earliest attention. The See of Canterbury was vacant by death. Here there could be no question of intrusion, and on the appointment to the primatial See the greatest issues manifestly depended. There was one divine for whom the Queen had an especial affection, and who was also well known to and much honoured by her leading ministers. This was Matthew Parker, who had been chaplain to her mother and her father, and, in King Edward's time, Dean of Lincoln. Parker had been named first in the Commission for revising the Prayer-book, and had he been able to attend, it is probable that the Queen's wishes would have been more carefully regarded He was known to be a moderate man; studious, well learned and upright; an able preacher; and seemed indeed to unite in himself all the qualities needed for a primate at this important juncture. But, on the other hand, he was in feeble health, had led a studious and retired life, and he himself unfeignedly shrank from the arduous task which the Queen desired to impose upon him. His resistance was at length with difficulty overcome. On July 18 (1559), the congé-d'élire was sent to the Chapter of Canterbury, with a letter missive nominating Parker. The Chapter were

The new bishops. Archbishop Parker

divided in their views; but at length they agreed to elect by way of compromise, leaving the actual election to the Dean, who duly elected Parker (August 1). On September 9 a Commission under the Great Seal was issued to certain bishops to consecrate him. But as the three first named of these refused to act, a second Commission was issued (December 6) to Kitchen, Bishop of Llandaff; Barlow, late Bishop of Bath and Wells; Scory, late Bishop of Chichester; Coverdale, late Bishop of Exeter; John, Suffragan of Bedford; John, Suffragan of Thetford; John Bale, late Bishop of Ossory, empowering them, or any four of them, to act. Kitchen, fearful, as is said, of Bonner's anathema, feared to act. The next four named in the Commission consented.

The election was confirmed on December 9 ; and on Sunday, December 17, Parker was consecrated accord-
His consecration ing to the ordinal of the Church of England, in the chapel of Lambeth Palace, by Bishops Barlow, Scory, Coverdale and Hodgkins. Of these bishops the two first had been consecrated in the time of Henry VIII., Coverdale in that of Edward VI. An absurd story, invented by the Romanists some fifty years later, endeavoured to throw discredit upon Parker's consecration, by pretending that it was done at a tavern in a ludicrous manner. It is enough to say that no historical fact is more fully and satisfactorily attested than the due and orderly performance of the ceremony. Then it has been attempted to throw doubts on the consecration of Bishop Barlow, who acted as the head of the Commission. Of this, however, the fullest proof can be given, though it happens that his consecration is not entered in Cranmer's register. But this register,

which was very carelessly kept, in like manner does not contain entries of the consecration of Gardiner, Fox, and some six or seven other prelates who are known to have been consecrated during Cranmer's primacy.

The Church of England had thus happily again a Primate; and he was now free to provide himself with Consecra- a body of suffragans who might ordain the tion of other bishops clergy needed in their several dioceses. In his first consecration, Grindal was made Bishop of London, Cox of Ely, Sandys of Worcester, and Merick of Bangor. Shortly afterwards Young was consecrated to the See of St. David's, Bullingham to Lincoln, Jewel to Salisbury, Davis to St. Asaph, and Guest to Rochester. The next month Barkley was consecrated to Bath and Wells, and Bentham to Lichfield and Coventry.

The new prelates were not altogether in an enviable position. The Sees had been robbed of their manors Poverty of under Henry VIII. and Edward VI., and the Sees after the death of Queen Mary, when the Popish bishops foresaw that their reign would be short, they had carefully set themselves to deplete their Sees as much as possible. 'They would rather give their manors to women, children, housekeepers (to say no worse), by lease, patents, annuities, than that any that loved God should enjoy them. Many bishoprics of the realm had they impoverished by these means, so that some of the new bishops had scarce a corner of a house to lie in; and divers not so much ground as to graze a goose or a sheep, so that some were compelled to tether their horses in their orchard.' In the midst of the great calls for active ministrations which pressed upon the prelates, this state of things was doubly unfortunate.

Ordinations of priests now quickly succeeded one another. On December 22 (1559) Bishop Scory, acting under a Commission from Bishop Parker, ordained at Lambeth eleven deacons and ten deacons and priests together, conferring both orders on the same day. These were for various dioceses. The Bishop of Bangor held an ordination on January 7, and in addition to some ordinations to the priesthood ordained five *readers*. On February 11 and March 3 there were more ordinations at Lambeth; and on March 10 the Bishop of Lincoln, acting under a Commission from the Primate, ordained 120 deacons, thirty-seven priests, and seven to both orders. Several other ordinations followed; but with all this the supply fell lamentably short of the demand.

Ordinations of clergy

Under these circumstances the bishops, under the Primate's direction, ordained as readers tradesmen or other unlearned persons so long as they were of good repute; the intention being that they should merely read the Service and the Homilies and perform some of the other church offices, but not administer the Sacraments. But this 'minor order,' which was intended to meet the present distress, was soon found not to be a successful arrangement. Before the end of the year the Archbishop had determined to abandon it. In August (1560) Parker writes to Grindal: 'Whereas occasioned by the great want of ministers, we and you both, for tolerable supply thereof, have heretofore admitted unto the ministry sundry artificers and others, not traded and brought up in

Ordination of readers

learning; and as it happened in a multitude, some that were of base occupations; forasmuch as now by experience it is seen that such manner of men, partly by reason of their former profane arts, partly by their light behaviour otherwise and trade of life, are very offensive to the people, yea, and to the wise of this realm are thought to do a great deal more hurt than good; the Gospel thus sustaining slander—these shall be to desire and require you hereafter to be very circumspect in admitting any to the ministry, and only to allow such as, having good testimony of their honest conversation, have been traded and exercised in learning, or at the least have spent their time with teaching of children; excluding all others which have been brought up and sustained themselves either by occupation or other kinds of life alienated from learning. This we pray you diligently to look unto, and to observe not only in your own person, but also to signify this our advertisement to other of our brethren, bishops of our province, in as good speed as ye may, so that you and they may stay from collating such orders to so unmeet persons, unto such time as in a Convocation we may meet together and have further conference thereof.'

The need, however, being very pressing, the Archbishop wisely determined to employ the same class of men without giving them orders, and thus making them a permanent burden upon the Church. He arranged for the temporary union of several benefices under an ordained minister, 'deputing in every parish committed to his care one able minister within the orders of deacon, if it may be, or else some

Arrangement for lay readers

honest and grave layman who, as a lector or reader, shall give his attendance to read the order of service appointed; except that he shall not, being only a reader, intermeddle with christening, marrying, or ministering the Holy Communion, or with any voluntary preaching or prophesying, but read the service of the day with the Litany and Homily, agreeably, as shall be prescribed, in the absence of the principal pastor, or some one pastor chanceably coming to that parish for the time.' The pastor was to make his circuit of the parishes constantly, administer the sacraments and oversee the work of the readers. These were to be appointed with consent of the bishop, and to be removable upon proof of disability and disorder. But while the Archbishop was thus striving with some success to provide ministers in the various parts of his province, he had to contend with a considerable difficulty in the narrow-minded scrupulousness of some of his brethren. The Queen insisted on retaining in her chapel the crucifix, lights, and vestments. Neither had she any great liking for sermons. A chorus of complaints goes forth from the new bishops to their friends abroad. Sampson, a man well qualified by learning and power, refused a bishopric on this ground. 'What can I hope for,' he writes pathetically, 'when the ministry of Christ is banished from Court, while the image of the Crucified is allowed with lights burning before it? when three of our lately appointed bishops are to officiate at the table of the Lord, one as priest, another as deacon, and a third as sub-deacon, before the image of the crucifix, and habited in the golden vestments of the Papacy, and are thus to

Scrupulousness of the new bishops

celebrate the Lord's Supper without any sermon?' Cox, Bishop of Ely, writes: 'We are constrained, to our great distress of mind, to tolerate in our churches the image of the cross and Him who was crucified.' Bishop Jewel writes: 'Matters are come to that: either the crosses of silver and tin which we have everywhere broken in pieces must be restored, or our bishoprics relinquished.' Bishop Sandys: 'I was rather vehement in the matter, and could by no means consent that an occasion of stumbling to the Church of Christ, so that I was very near being deposed from my office and incurring the displeasure of the Queen. . . . The Popish vestments remain in our Church, I mean the copes, which however we hope will not last very long.' It was no doubt seriously deliberated upon by many in high place whether they were not called upon rather to abandon their position than to countenance the enforcement of any sort of decent ceremonial. With such half-hearted coadjutors, the Archbishop had no easy task before him when he set himself to perform the great work which the Queen specially required at his hands, namely, the enforcement of order and discipline.

CHAPTER XVII.

THE DISCIPLINE.

1559–1571.

THE way for the action of the bishops had been prepared by a royal visitation, following the precedents of the two previous reigns. The Queen, by virtue of her ecclesiastical supremacy, had reissued the Injunctions of the first year of Edward, with certain additions which were thought to be necessitated by the state of things then existing.

Queen Elizabeth's Injunctions

The most characteristic of these additions is perhaps the twenty-ninth Injunction, which treats of clerical matrimony. It is said that the Injunctions were drawn up by the same set of divines as revised the Prayer-book. Whether this were so or not, there is pretty clear internal evidence that the Injunction as to matrimony proceeded from the Queen herself. It is well known that Elizabeth was strongly opposed to the marriage of the clergy; her spite against it, and desire to pour contempt upon it, break out in this Injunction in a somewhat scandalous manner. 'Because,' it is said, 'there hath grown offence and some slander to the Church by lack of discreet and sober behaviour in many ministers of the Church, both in choosing their wives and in discreet living with them, the remedy whereof is necessary to be sought; it is thought, therefore, very necessary that no manner of priest or deacon shall hereafter take to his wife any manner of woman, without the advice and allowance first had, upon good examination, by the bishop of the same diocese, and two justices of peace of the same shire, dwelling next to the place where the same woman hath made her most abode before the marriage; nor without the good-will of the parents of the said woman, if she have any living, or two of the next of her kinsfolks, or for lack of knowledge of such, of her master and mistress where she serveth. And before he shall be contracted in any place, he shall make a good

Clerical matrimony

and certain proof hereof to the minister or to the congregation assembled for that purpose, which shall be upon some holy day where divers may be present. And if any shall do otherwise, that then they shall not be permitted to minister either the word or sacraments of the Church, nor shall be capable of any ecclesiastical benefice.' The contemptuous spite against clerical matrimony which may be read in this Injunction was displayed in many other acts and utterances of the Queen. Archbishop Parker was so grieved by it, that he declared that it had made him bitterly regret his ever having accepted office at her desire.

Another Injunction in which the Queen's special views are represented is the twenty-fifth, which repeats the earlier Injunction of King Edward touching images, without reference to the Injunction published soon after through Cranmer, that all images should be removed from churches. In this Injunction nothing is said as to the removal, but only the 'decking' of them is forbidden. The people indeed proceeded in many places to remove them, and the Queen caused dismay among her bishops by declaring that she would have them reinstated. Upon this a formal address was presented to the Queen by some of the bishops whose consciences were aggrieved, which, after quoting many authorities against the use of images, concludes, 'We beseech your Majesty, in these and such like controversies of religion, to refer the discussment and deciding of them to a synod of bishops, and other godly learned men, according to the example of Constantinus Magnus and other Christian emperors, and to consider, that besides weighty causes in policy, the establishing of

Images in churches

images by your authority shall not only utterly discredit our ministries, but also blemish the fame of your most godly brother, and such notable fathers as have given their lives for the testimony of God's truth, who by public law removed all images.' The Queen was persuaded to withdraw the order for their restitution, but nevertheless she still retained the crucifix in her own chapel. In these Injunctions there are valuable directions for reverence in divine service; for the careful and orderly change of the altar into a table, when it was thought necessary, but at the same time it is said, 'there seemeth no matter of great moment' why the change should be made; for the use in the Holy Communion of round wafers instead of common bread, and for a 'modest and distinct song' in the using the Common Prayer.

But the most satisfactory part of the document is the 'admonition to simple men deceived by the malicious,' in which an explanation of what was meant by the 'ecclesiastical supremacy' is given. 'Her Majesty neither doth, nor ever will, challenge any [other] authority, than under God to have the sovereignty and rule over all manner of persons born within these her realms, dominions, and countries, of what estate, either ecclesiastical or temporal soever they be, so as no other foreign powers shall or ought to have any superiority over them.' The Queen utterly repudiates the sentiments of those who 'most sinisterly and maliciously labour to notify to her loving subjects how by words of the said oath it may be collected that the kings or queens of this realm, possessors of the Crown, may challenge authority and power of ministry

Exp'anation of the Royal Supremacy

of divine service in the Church.' This wholesome doctrine of the Supremacy was afterwards fully embodied in the Articles of Religion; and in accordance with this the Queen in the bidding prayer is described not as 'the supreme head immediately under God of the spiritualty and temporalty of the Church,' as Edward was, but as 'supreme governor of this realm in all causes ecclesiastical as temporal.'

The bidding prayer of Edward is further changed by the omission of the bidding of prayer for the dead.

Prayer for the dead In place of this is substituted, 'Let us praise God for all those that are departed out of this life in the faith of Christ,' and pray 'that we, with them, be made partakers of the glorious resurrection.' The Injunctions having been issued, a number of articles of inquiry were framed upon them, which were to be administered by various bodies of Commissioners throughout the country.

The Commission for the northern province provided for the allowance of pensions to the ministers ejected *Visitation of the Commissioners* for refusing to conform. Part of the duties of the Commissioners was to provide sermons.

At Auckland they were anxious to procure the services of Bernard Gilpin, the famous apostle of the north, *Bernard Gilpin* who, though accepting reforming views, had lived in all amity with Bishop Tonstal in the diocese of Durham, and was held in universal respect. Gilpin was somewhat doubtful about advocating the proceedings of the Commissioners, but at length he consented to preach against the primacy of the Pope. Finding, however, that Dr. Sandys, preaching the previous day, had argued against the doctrine of the real presence in the Eucharist, Gilpin again hesitated as to subscription. His scruples were at length overcome, principally on the ground that if he refused to subscribe almost all the clergy in the north would be sure to follow his example. He subscribed, therefore, to the declaration tendered by the Commissioners, but at the same time he did not fail to send to Dr. Sandys a protest against his doctrine. In the London visitation the roods and images were generally pulled down and burned, which was the cause of the anger of the Queen which has been mentioned.

The Commissioners tendered to the clergy the declaration as follows: 'We do confess and acknowledge the restoration again of the ancient jurisdiction over the state ecclesiastical and temporal of this realm of England, and abolishing of all foreign power repugnant to the same, according to an act thereof made in the last Parliament; the administration of the sacraments, the use and order of divine service, in manner and form as it is set forth in a book commonly called "The Book of Common Prayer," established by the same act (? Parliament), and the orders and rules contained in the Injunctions given by the Queen's Majesty, and exhibited in this present visitation, to be according to the true word of God, and agreeable with the doctrine and use of the primitive and apostolic Church. In witness whereof hereunto we have subscribed our names.' The number of the clergy ejected under this visitation has been already mentioned. The Queen by her Commissioners had thus prepared the way for the action of the bishops; but when they were once constituted, the enforcement of discipline was to be left to them.

The declaration

Archbishop Parker, recognising this, at once proceeded to take counsel with some of his brethren as to the way in which the Injunctions were to be carried out, and the difficulties of the position. There were strong objections on the part of some of the clergy to the clerical dress prescribed to be used in the Church ministrations and in ordinary life. There was also the difficulty caused by the absence of any test of fitness, of doctrine, or of competent knowledge on the part of those who were willing to subscribe the formula of acceptance. The resolutions of the bishops were cast into the form of a paper headed 'Interpretations and further considerations,' a copy of which remains among the Primate's papers. It is a sort of comment upon certain of the Injunctions, indicating the way in which they were to be enforced by the bishops. Whatever force it had depended upon the authority belonging to the Injunctions. Some of the notes show a desire for a more lenient code than that expressed in the Injunctions. Thus incumbents may satisfy the requirements of the law by preaching once a quarter instead of once a month. Some express a greater strictness. Thus curates are to be made to learn to repeat certain texts. No shops were to be kept open on Sundays, and at fairs 'no showing of merchandise till service be done.' 'All bishops and others having any living ecclesiastical, to go in apparel agreeable, or else with'n two monitions given by the ordinary to be deposed or sequestered from his fruits.' 'Incorrigible Arians, Pelagians, and Free-will men to be sent into some one castle in North Wales, or Wallingford, and there to live of their own labour and exercise.' With regard to the Church service it is recommended that 'there be used but one apparel; as the cope in the ministration of the Lord's Supper and the surplice in all other ministrations, and that there be no other manner and form of ministering the sacraments but as the Service-book doth precisely prescribe, with the declaration of the Injunctions, as, for example, the common bread.' This resolution may be regarded as aimed at the laxer section. The next seems directed against the other side. 'That the table be removed out of the choir into the body of the church before the chancel door, where either the choir seemeth to be too little, or at great feasts of receivings, and at the end of the communion to be set up again according to the Injunctions.' The Injunction allowed the Holy Table, which was to stand 'where the altar stood,' to be moved as occasion required *within the chancel*. This comment authorises it to be moved out of the chancel, thereby emphasising the Zwinglian notion of the Holy Communion being a commemorative feast. Other provisions of the same character with regard to the Sacraments follow, and some useful rules of discipline as to admission to orders and collation to benefices.

But the most important work of this little episcopal synod was to agree upon certain articles of religion to be proposed to all ministers on entering a benefice, and to draw up a *declaration* in English, grounded upon these, which the ministers were to read and subscribe. This was the best provision which the Archbishop could devise for bringing about a unity in doctrine of the ministering clergy. And for the bishops he drew up a short paper, recommending that the licences granted by the Visitors should be no longer in force, but that the bishops should examine the clergy for themselves as to their competency, and that the clergy should in their preaching set out the 'reverend estimation of the holy sacraments of Baptism and the Lord's Supper; exciting the people to the often and devout receiving of the body and blood of Christ in such form as is already prescribed in the Book of Common Prayer.' Public baptism should be ministered in the font, 'not in basons or other like thing.' Private baptism, when in peril of death, might be used either by the minister 'or some other grave and sober person.' A proclamation issued about this time against defacing monuments in churches, under the pretence of doing away with superstitious memorials, is also supposed to have been drawn up by the pen of the Archbishop, who, in union with the Queen, was doing his best to establish in the reformed Church of England a comely and decent ritual, with due reverence and ceremonial.

But it must be confessed that Parker had but little assistance in this matter from the bishops and clergy with whom he had to work. It would seem as though the enormities of that Church which had always upheld and practised a splendid ceremonial worship, had completely alienated the reformed clergy from anything approaching to its model. They connected decent ceremonies and rites with blasphemous doctrines and murderous persecutions, and altogether shrank from them. Their friends and supporters in the foreign reformed communities had thrown off all these things; why should not they be equally free and happy? Thus, to many, every sort of clerical

The bishops not favourable to the discipline

The Discipline

vesture, even the simplest, was an abomination; every attempt to restrict ministers from following their own fancies in the celebration of divine worship was a tyranny. The irregularities which were everywhere apparent angered the Queen beyond measure, and the Archbishop had by no means a happy time in trying to satisfy Her Majesty by reducing the 'Germanical natures,' as he called them, of the clergy to some sort of order.

Under these circumstances he probably rejoiced to be able to summon his Provincial Synod (January 19, 1563). But he must have been grievously disappointed when he encountered in that Synod an organised attempt to overset the little discipline which had as yet been established. A paper signed by thirty-two members of the Lower House prayed the Synod to resolve: (1) against the chanting of the Psalms with the organ accompaniment; (2) against the use of the Cross in baptism; (3) to leave kneeling at the communion discretionary; (4) that copes and surplices be discontinued; (5) that the clerical dress for ordinary use be abandoned; (6) that all saints' days and holidays 'bearing the name of a creature, may, as leading to superstition, or rather gentility, be clearly abrogated.' Resolutions embodying these demands in a slightly modified form were proposed to the House (February 13), and a great debate followed. 'Those,' says Strype, 'who were for alterations and for stripping the English Church of her ceremonies and usages then retained and used, were such (as I find by their names subscribed) as had lately lived abroad in the reformed churches of Geneva, Switzerland, or Germany. But the divines on

Debate on ceremonies in the Convocation

the other side reckoned the wisdom, learning, and piety of Cranmer, Ridley, and the other reformers of the Church, to be equal every way with those of the foreign reformers, and knew what these venerable men did in the settlement of this Church was accompanied with great deliberation, and a resolution of reducing it in doctrine and worship to the platform of the primitive churches, as they found it in the old ecclesiastical writers.' This party ultimately succeeded in negativing the resolutions, but only by a majority of *one*. With such a difference of opinion among the leading clergy, it is not to be wondered at that the greatest absence of uniformity and the most contradictory uses should prevail in the celebration of divine service. The bishops were no more of one mind than the clergy, and in some dioceses there was no attempt made to enforce ritual, conformity, or decency of ceremonial.

Under these circumstances the Queen addressed to the Primate a letter, dated January 25, 1565. After speaking severely of the state of disorder in the Church, and reflecting sharply upon the Primate and bishops for not rectifying it, the Queen proceeds : 'Therefore we do by these our present letters require, enjoin, and straitly charge you, being the Metropolitan, according to the power and authority which you have under us over this province of Canterbury (as the like we will order for the province of York), to confer with the bishops your brethren, namely, such as be in commission for causes ecclesiastical . . . and cause to be truly understood what varieties, novelties, and diversities there are in our clergy, or among our people, either in doctrine or in

The Queen's letter to the Primate

ceremonies and rights of the Church, or in the manners, usages, and behaviour of the clergy themselves, by what name soever any of them be called. And, thereupon, as the several cases shall appear to require reformation, so to proceed by order, injunction, or censure, according to the order and appointment of such laws and ordinances as are provided by Act of Parliament and the true meaning thereof. And for the time to come we will and straitly charge to provide and enjoin in our name, in all and every place of your province, that none hereafter be admitted to any place ecclesiastical but such as shall be found advisedly given to common order in all external rites and ceremonies, both for the Church and their own persons. And if any superior officers be found hereunto disagreeable, to inform us hereof. For we intend to have no dissension or variety grow, by suffering of persons which maintain the same to remain in authority.' Upon receiving this letter Archbishop Parker wrote to the Bishop of London to communicate to the other bishops of the province Her Majesty's wishes, and also to desire them to furnish him with a report as to the state of conformity in their dioceses.

Upon the receipt of these reports Parker drew up what he calls a 'Book of Articles,' put together by himself and several other bishops, and this he sent to Secretary Cecil for approval. He was desirous that the Queen should authorise these Articles and enforce them by her royal authority, but this she would not do. She had indeed issued a body of Injunctions in an abnormal state of the Church, when *as yet there were no bishops*; but now that bishops

Archbishop Parker's Advertisements

existed with full authority, it was their business to enforce order, not hers. The Archbishop was much vexed at this answer; but he altered his 'Book of Articles,' and again next year endeavoured to obtain the Queen's authorisation. At the same time he said that, failing this, he was fully determined 'to prosecute this order,' and as the Queen would 'needs have him assay with his own authority,' he trusts 'that he shall not be stayed hereafter.' The new Rules were therefore now published by him (March 1566) as 'Advertisements, partly for due order in the public ministration of Common Prayers and using the Holy Sacraments, and partly for the apparel of all persons ecclesiastical by virtue of the Queen's Majesty's letters commanding the same, January 25.' Under this last head it is directed that in cathedrals, at ministration of Holy Communion, the 'principal minister shall use a cope, with gospeller and epistler agreeably;' but in parish churches the minister at all ministrations 'shall wear a comely surplice with sleeves.' This was an abandonment of the attempt to enforce the use of the cope in parish churches, which had been contemplated in the 'Interpretations' of a few years previously. So general was the opposition to clerical vestments, that now a permissible minimum is specified. Communicants are enjoined to receive kneeling. Fonts are to be used for baptism. The holidays of the 'new calendar authorised by the Queen' are to be observed, and many other disciplinary regulations. As regards the ordinary dress of the clergy, the bishops are to wear their accustomed dress. Dignified clergy to wear a side-gown with sleeves cut straight at the hands, a tippet

The Discipline

(scarf) of sarsenet. Other 'ecclesiastical persons' to wear the same shaped gown, and square cap, without tippet. Poor clergy might wear short gowns.

These directions as to dress can scarcely be considered onerous, merely prescribing, as they do, a simple linen garment for church ministrations, and a black gown and cap for ordinary use. Nevertheless they excited the most violent opposition in a section of the clergy. The Archbishop and some of the other bishops, having the power of the Ecclesiastical Commission, were able to punish breaches of discipline with fine and imprisonment; but still the opposition raged fiercely. The London ministers were especially unconformable. Soon after the publication of the 'Advertisements' they made a sort of reply, called 'A Declaration of the doings of those ministers of God's Word and Sacraments in the city of London, which have refused to wear the upper apparel and ministering garments of the Pope's Church.' In this book they show 'that neither the Prophets in the Old Testament, nor the Apostles in the New, were distinguished by their garments; that the linen garment was peculiar to the priesthood of Aaron, and had a signification of something to be fulfilled in Christ and His Church. That the surplice or white linen garment came from the Egyptians into the Jewish Church, and that Pope Sylvester, about the year 320, was the first that appointed the Sacrament to be administered in a white linen garment, giving this reason for it—because the body of Christ was buried in a white linen cloth. These garments have been abused to idolatry, sorcery, and all

marginal notes: Opposition of some of the clergy. Reply of the London ministers kinds of conjurations; for (say they) the Popish priests can perform none of their pretended consecrations of holy water, transubstantiation of the body of Christ, conjurations of the devil out of places or persons possessed, without a surplice, or an albe, or some hallowed stole. The habits are an offence to weak Christians, an encouragement to ignorant and obstinate Papists, and an affectation to return to their communion.'

Such were some of the grounds on which these men persuaded themselves that it was incumbent on them to resist authority and to sacrifice the peace of the Church. The controversy which began about vestments speedily passed on to other things—Church government, discipline, and forms of prayer. The name of *Puritans* now first began to be applied to those who scrupled about the Church ceremonial. Some of these soon determined to separate from the Church and to hold secret and unlawful assemblies for worship. Others remained in the Church, endeavouring to elude conformity by every art and stratagem—thorns in the sides of the bishops, who were ever being driven onward by the Queen to repress their eccentricities; in some parts of the reign a source of most serious danger to the Church of England, until at length reduced by Whitgift, and refuted by Hooker. In the Parliaments of 1571-2, the Puritanical element had considerable power, and had the Queen been less firm and resolute it might even have triumphed. It is, however, very noteworthy, and very admirable, that all attempts to give a Puritanical character to the Church of England, either in doctrine or discipline, have universally failed, though sometimes their success has seemed very near. Thus

Growth and ill effects of the controversy

Alexander Nowel's Catechism, though almost accepted by Convocation, was never quite sanctioned. The new book of discipline, 'Reformatio legum ecclesiasticarum,' though three times coming near to the receiving of the royal ratification, never did receive it, and at last completely disappeared. The various schemes for upsetting the Prayer-book in the time of Elizabeth all miscarried. But though a member of the Church of England may fairly rejoice at the failure of the dangerous and threatening attacks of the ultra-Reformers, it does not follow from this that he must needs approve of all the methods by which this was brought about. The Court of High Commission, which was the great instrument for subduing Puritanism, was an institution alien from the spirit of our laws, and its procedure by the method of objecting articles, and requiring purgation upon oath, was charged with gross injustice. It would be impossible to defend all the acts of the reign of Elizabeth, either in Church or State, on the ground of principle. Necessity and the difficulties of the time can alone be pleaded. The treatment of the Romanist missionaries, after the excommunicating Bull of the Pope, has many terrible chapters. In the period, however, covered by this history, there was not much cause of complaint as regards the Romanists. Persons and Cresswell in their memorial to the Queen acknowledge, 'In the beginning of thy kingdom thou didst deal something more gently with Catholics. None were then urged by thee or pressed either to thy sect or to the denial of the faith. All things did seem to proceed in a far milder course. No great complaints were heard of.' And the body of secular priests in England, who in 1601 published their views, go so far as to say, 'None were ever vexed that way and simply for that he was either priest or Catholic, but because they were suspected to have had their hands in some of the said most traitorous designments.' There is indeed abundant evidence to prove that, up to the time of the papal excommunication of Elizabeth in 1570, the Romanists attended the service of the Church of England, and showed a temper altogether different from that which they displayed after the coming of the seminary priests. From that time Romanism was intensely hostile to the Church of England; and with these powerful enemies on one side, and the equally fierce and more numerous Puritans on the other; the hollow loyalty of the nonconforming clergy; the bitter and libellous attacks of the Anabaptists, Familists, and Brownists, it was no small evidence of power in the Church of England that it went on gathering strength and comeliness until it reached an era of partial repose in the latter days of the great Queen.

CHAPTER XVIII.

THE DOCTRINAL CONFESSION.

1563-1571.

IT MAY perhaps be considered somewhat strange that the doctrinal confession contained in the forty-two articles published in the time of Edward VI. was not restored by the same authority which restored the Prayer-book.

THE DOCTRINAL CONFESSION

But the Queen was by no means so well inclined to accept the reformed doctrine as she was to re-establish the Service-book, and to enforce discipline. It was her policy and her hope to include at least the more moderate section of the Romanists within the Church, and she desired no sharp delimitations of doctrine which should effectually exclude them. Thus for the first four years of her reign there was no doctrinal standard for the English Church beyond that which was contained in the Prayer-book. The bishops had indeed found it necessary to put forth a short form, contained in eleven articles which were to be accepted by the clergy; but these had no legal or binding character,[1] and were not ratified by the Queen. It is probable that the general acceptance of the Reformation settlement in the country, and the little opposition offered to the Archbishop's measures, except by a few of the more contentious of the clergy, induced the Queen to sanction the reintroduction of the longer doctrinal confession.

The doctrinal confession not restored at first

But this was not to be done without a careful review such as that to which the Prayer-book had been subjected. The preliminary part of this work was undertaken by the Primate, Bishops Cox and Guest, in the autumn and early winter of 1562. The MS. of the forty-two articles subjected to this review has been preserved; and it is found that as the original articles were drawn in great measure from the

Review of the forty-two articles

---

[1] These eleven articles were legalised for the Church of Ireland, and constituted the sole formulary of that Church till 1615. But in England they were intended merely as a provisional test of orthodoxy.—*Hardwick*.

Confession of Augsburg, so the new matter now introduced was borrowed extensively from another Lutheran Confession, that of Würtemberg. But in addition to this, numerous changes were introduced to meet developments of doctrine which had sprung up since the first drafting of the articles, and much was cut off which was deemed superfluous. 'The effect of this searching criticism of Parker and his colleagues,' says Hardwick, ' was, first, to add four articles; secondly, to take away an equal number; thirdly, to modify by partial amplification or curtailment as many as seventeen of the remainder.'

The Convocation of Canterbury, after the preliminary formalities, began its work on the articles on January 19 (1563). The Upper House agreed to and signed them on January 29. The articles were reduced to thirty-nine, by omitting three relating to the theories of Anabaptism. An important alteration was also made in the article on the Lord's Supper, the former expressions having been thought to favour the Zwinglian doctrine; and, with some other changes, the document was sent down to the Lower House. It seems to have been considered by the bishops that a very short time was sufficient for the consideration of the formula by that body. On February 5 the document with subscriptions was called for. A good many of the members of the Lower House had, however, demurred about subscribing, and the Prolocutor asked the President that they should be ordered to subscribe. On February 10 it was reported to the bishops that some still refused. The majority, however, certainly subscribed, and the document as agreed upon by Convocation was forwarded to the Queen for ratification.

But it was a long time before this was given, and when at length the Latin copy of the articles with the Queen's ratification appeared, it was found to have two important variations from the copy which had been agreed upon and signed in Convocation. Very much the same, apparently, had been done by the Queen in Council as was done by her with regard to the Prayer-book. An article which denied that the wicked were in any wise partakers of the Lord's Supper—article twenty-nine—thus seeming to invalidate the doctrine of the real presence—was struck out, and a clause was added to the twentieth article which asserted that 'the Church hath power to decree rites and ceremonies, and authority in controversies of faith.'

The Queen's ratification

A great controversy has arisen about this clause. In the English copy, printed soon after the Latin one which bears the Queen's ratification, it does not appear. It was afterwards charged against Archbishop Laud that he had inserted the clause without authority; but there is abundant evidence that it had its place in the copy of the articles which was finally ratified and subscribed in 1571.

The clause in the twentieth article

An attempt was made in Parliament in 1566 to carry an Act making subscription to the articles binding on all the clergy. The copy of the articles which was specified in the Bill was the English version of 1563, which did not contain the clause inserted by the Queen, nor the twenty-ninth article. Whether it was owing to the omission of this clause, or to the strong dislike which the Queen always felt to

Attempt to enforce subscription by law

Parliament intermeddling in the affairs of religion, this Bill, having passed the Commons, was 'abruptly stayed' by the Queen's command in the House of Lords. This was greatly to the annoyance of the bishops, who were continually striving to obtain secular authority for their discipline, and were unwilling to exert their ecclesiastical authority as much as the Queen desired. They seem even to have apprehended that the Queen by 'staying' the Bill was inclined to withdraw her support from the articles altogether; and they complain that ' for want of a plain certainty of articles of doctrine by law to be declared, great distraction and dissention of minds is at this present among your subjects, and daily is like more and more to increase, and that with very great danger in policy, the circumstances considered, if the said book of articles be now stayed in your Majesty's hand, or (as God forbid) rejected.' There is no reason to suppose that Queen Elizabeth had any special affection for the articles; but she had no intention of rejecting them. She considered she had done quite sufficient for their establishment by her ratification. But as it was well known that many of the incumbents of livings held Romanising views, the desire to have subscription to the articles enforced by Act of Parliament was the favourite policy of the Puritan party, as well as of the bishops, while to the Queen, who did not desire at that time to bear hard upon the Romanists, it was distasteful. By the time of the Parliament of 1571, however, both this party had grown in strength, and the Queen, after the northern rebellion and her excommunication by the Pope, regarded matters differently.

In May 1571, an Act was passed by both Houses of Parliament and received the royal assent, which enacted that all the clergy should, before Christmas next, in the presence of their Ordinaries, subscribe the Book of the Articles of Religion, 'which only concern the confession of the true Christian faith and the doctrine of the Sacraments.' It was argued afterwards that this Act did not make subscription compulsory as to any other articles besides those which concerned faith and doctrine. But it was the judgment of Sir E. Coke that the word *only* was not intended to divide the articles, but to qualify or describe the whole of them. No doubt at this time the Queen's anger was great against the Romanising party, against whom the Subscription Bill was specially aimed; but it must have cost her a considerable effort to depart thus from her favourite policy, and to make such a concession to the Puritanical party in Parliament.

The Act of 1571

This agitation on the subject of the articles in Parliament was the cause of renewed attention being paid to them in the Convocation of 1571. Those who had not subscribed them in 1563 were now, if still Members of the House, peremptorily ordered to subscribe under pain of excommunication. One bishop, Cheyney of Gloucester, refused subscription, and was actually excommunicated, though soon restored on subscription. The articles were carefully revised and the change made by the Queen in the twentieth article was now accepted. On the other hand the twenty-ninth article was restored; and this form was subscribed by Convocation. The revised English edition was to be superintended and edited by

The Articles finally revised by the Convocation of 1571

Bishop Jewel. This contained the disputed clause of the twentieth article, and had some other emendations of the 1563 copy, but made no important change. It was to this copy that the whole of the clergy were now called upon to affix their signatures; and this subscription was strictly enforced and carried out by the order of Convocation, and the action of the Ecclesiastical Commissioners. Thus the subscription was, as it were, taken by the Church out of the domain of the Act of Parliament; and the acceptance not only of the doctrinal articles but of all the articles indifferently was made compulsory.

It is clear that, fairly considered, the affixing a signature to a long doctrinal confession is not equivalent to an assertion that the signer admits and believes every statement in that confession, but only that he accepts it as a whole, and undertakes not to teach doctrine contrariant to it. Viewed in this light, subscription to the doctrinal confession of 1563 seems nothing more than the authorities in Church and State were justified in demanding of the clergy; and there can be no question that this subscription has been of the highest value in preserving a uniform standard of doctrine in the Church of England.

Character of the subscription

The same may doubtless be said in a lesser degree of the homilies which were now set forth, in addition to those which had been published in King Edward's time. The authorship of these is generally attributed to Cox, Bishop of Ely, who had so considerable a share in compiling the Prayer-book of King Edward's reign, and in reviewing and recasting the articles. The Queen, ever opposed to doctrinal

The new homilies

statements, made a difficulty about sanctioning the homilies, as she had done about the articles.

This, however, was ultimately overcome, and with the work of the Convocation of 1571 the Reformation settlement of the Church of England may be regarded as complete. Much still indeed remained to be done in the way of discipline and organisation, and specially in the providing a sufficiency of preachers, which was the great want of the Church for many years. But the lines had been laid down, the framework constructed, and the way made plain for further progress. England had effectually broken with the Pope, who had excommunicated her Queen and was endeavouring to raise up enemies on every side. She had learnt by the reign of Mary what a return to the subjection to Rome meant, and there was no fear of her again making the experiment. Freed from external tyranny and slavish bonds, the national Church could now go forward in security and peace to perfect her system, and to bring forth from her bosom that great body of learned and eloquent divines, which has availed to make the Church of England a praise upon earth.

Completion of the Reformation settlement

CHAPTER XIX.

THE DEFENCE OF THE REFORMATION.

ALL through the Middle Ages the Church of England had been constantly protesting against Rome. The extortion, corruption, and tyranny of the Court of

Rome and of the Pope, its head, were the theme of constant invectives. Some, as Bishop Grosseteste, had gone so far as to speak of the Pope as antiChrist, and nothing was too bad for the satirists to allege against the whole Roman court. Yet for all this there had been no serious attempt to take the only step which could effectually free the Church from these mischiefs, viz., to withdraw from subjection to the See of Rome, and to assert and act upon the national independence of the Church. This policy had been frequently indicated, and lay at the root of numerous laws passed to restrain Roman encroachments; but it had never been fully carried out to its legitimate ends. The fiction of the supremacy of the Roman bishop, though without any foundation in primitive antiquity, had yet so fully entered into the mind of mediæval Europe, that it seemed as though it could not be effectually shaken. It was a fiction, moreover, eminently useful to kings and rulers, who by humouring it were able to obtain large subsidies from the clergy, and the nomination to all the richest preferments, dispensations to break vows and cast aside oaths, and licences to contract prohibited and even incestuous marriages.

Protests against Rome in earlier times

At length in England this very dispensing power —the fruitful parent of so much sin—was the cause of the alienation of the ruler of the land, and, under the protection of this prince, who was a monarch of exceptionally strong character, the clergy ventured to do what for a long time they had desired but feared to attempt, and proclaim the independence of the national Church. This, when fortified by Act of

At length successful

Parliament, was the foundation of the Reformation, and from this the remainder of its history naturally followed.

But as this step brought the Church of England into a position differing from that of the other churches of Europe, which still slavishly followed Rome, it was obvious that the Anglican Church, with its national life, would be violently assailed from all quarters which still kept fellowship with Rome, and would be pelted with the charges of schism and heresy, of Erastianism and profanity, and all the choice vocabulary of disappointed Inquisitors. Hence that Church needed vigorous defenders, who should not merely speak the language of meek apologetics, but who should be able to retort on the assailants with overwhelming power, and lay bare the manifold enormities both in doctrine and discipline which rendered separation from Rome absolutely necessary.

The cause of obloquy against the Church of England

The Church of England has been happy in having a succession of such defenders, whose labours have clearly established for all those who have the power or the desire to judge fairly, that in her Reformation the Church of England broke no church law, violated no authorised creed, sacrificed no true principle of unity, lost no essential of church life, but in a regular and canonical way threw off a load of superstition, and drew nearer to the practice of primitive antiquity.

Defenders of the English Church

The first of these defenders to be quoted was John Jewel, Bishop of Salisbury, who in 1562 published his famous apology for the Church of England—a work written in Latin, but quickly translated into English, and into all the European languages. At the conclusion of this work, which is a spirited invective against the Roman corruptions, the Bishop writes: 'We have departed from that Church which they had made a den of thieves, in which they had left nothing sound or like a Church, and which they themselves confessed to have erred in many things; as Lot left Sodom, or Abraham Chaldæa, not out of contention, but out of obedience to God; and have sought the certain way of religion out of the sacred Scriptures, which we know cannot deceive us, and have returned to the primitive Church of the ancient fathers and apostles, that is, to the beginning and first rise of the Church, as to the proper fountain. We have not indeed expected the authority or consent of the Council of Trent, in which we saw nothing was managed well and regularly; where all that entered took an oath to one man; where the ambassadors of our princes were despised and ill-treated; where none of our divines could be heard; where partiality and ambition openly carried all things; and, according to the practice of the holy fathers, and the customs of our own ancestors, we have reformed our churches in a provincial synod, and according to our duty have cast off the yoke and tyranny of the Bishop of Rome, who had no just authority over us, nor was like either Christ, or St. Peter, or the Apostles, or indeed like a bishop in anything. We do not decline concord and peace with men, but we will not continue in a state of war with God that we may have peace with men. If the Pope does indeed desire us to be reconciled to him, he ought first to reconcile himself to God. We know that all we teach is true,

Bishop Jewel

and we cannot offer violence to our own consciences, or give testimony against God, for if we deny any part of the Gospel of Jesus Christ before men, He will in like manner deny us before His Father; and if there be any that will be offended and cannot bear the doctrine of Christ, they are blind and the leaders of the blind; but the truth is still to be preached and owned, and we must patiently expect the judgment of God.'

The next witness to be quoted in defence of the Reformation is a divine of a different stamp and temper from the impetuous Jewel—the calm, learned, and judicious Richard Hooker. Hooker's great work was published about thirty years after that of Jewel. 'It is,' he writes, 'an error and misconceit wherewith they are possessed who ask us where our Church did lurk, in what cave of the earth it slept, for so many hundreds of years together before the birth of Martin Luther? As if we were of opinion that Luther did erect a new Church of Christ. No! the Church of Christ, which was from the beginning, is and continueth unto the end; of which Church all parts have not been equally sincere and sound. We hope that to reform ourselves, if at any time we have done amiss, is not to sever ourselves from the Church we were of before. The indisposition of the Church of Rome to reform herself must be no stay unto us from performing our duty to God; even as desire of retaining conformity with them could be no excuse if we did not perform that duty. Notwithstanding, so far as lawfully we may, we have held and do hold fellowship with them. We dare not communicate with Rome concerning sundry her gross and grievous abominations, yet touching those

Richard Hooker

main parts of Christian truth wherein they constantly still persist, we gladly acknowledge them to be of the family of Jesus Christ, and our hearty prayer unto God Almighty is, that being joined so far forth with them, they may at length (if it be His will) so yield to frame and reform themselves that no distraction remain in anything, but that we all may with one heart and one mouth glorify God, the Father of our Lord and Saviour, whose Church we are.'

This stock taunt of the Romanist as to the novelty of the Reformed Church of England, and the insulting question often thrown in the teeth of its members, 'Where was your Church before the days of Luther?' is also well answered by Dr. Field, Dean of Gloucester, in his work on the Church published soon after the work of Hooker. 'It is most fond and frivolous that some demand of us where our Church was before Luther began? For we say it was where it now is. If they ask us which? we answer it was the known and apparent Church in the world, wherein all our fathers lived and died, wherein Luther and the rest were baptized, received their Christianity, ordination, and power of ministry. If they reply that the Church was theirs and not ours, for that the doctrines they now teach and we impugn; the ceremonies, customs, and observations which they retain and defend, and we have abolished as fond, vain and superstitious, were taught, used, and practised in that Church wherein our fathers lived and died, we answer that none of these points of false doctrine and error, which they now maintain and we condemn, were the doctrines of that Church constantly delivered or generally received

[margin: Dean Field]

The Defence of the Reformation 205

by all them that were of it, but doubtfully broached and devised without all certain resolution, or factiously defended by some certain only, who as a dangerous faction adulterated the sincerity of the Christian verity, and brought the Church into miserable bondage. Touching the abuses and manifold superstitions which we have removed, it is true they were in the Church wherein our fathers lived, but not without signification of their dislike of them and earnest desire of reformation. So when many princes, prelates, and great states of the Church have in our days shaken off the yoke of miserable bondage whereof our fathers complained, removed these superstitious abuses they disliked, condemned those errors in matter of doctrine which they acknowledged to be dangerous and damnable, fretting as a canker and ensnaring the consciences of many, it is vain and frivolous for the patrons of error to ask us which and where our Church was before the Reformation began; for it was that wherein all our fathers lived, longing to see things brought back to their first beginnings again; in which their predecessors, as a dangerous and wicked faction, tyrannised over men's consciences, and perverted all things to the endless destruction of themselves and many others with whom they prevailed.'

The Church of England by the circumstances of its position was necessarily a controversial Church, and has been obliged to wage a vigorous war against many generations of opponents. It has produced many masters of controversy, but none perhaps more completely furnished with the necessary weapons than John Bramhall, Archbishop of Armagh, who waged vigorous war with enemies on every side. In

Archbishop Bramhall

one of the ablest of his treatises, 'A just vindication of the Church of England,' he thus pointedly states the case for the national rights of the English Church. 'Nothing hath been hitherto, or can hereafter be objected to the Church of England, which, to strangers unacquainted with the state of our affairs, or to such of our natives as have only looked upon the case superficially, hath more colour of truth, at first sight, than that of schism—that we have withdrawn our obedience from the Vicar of Christ, or at least from our lawful Patriarch, and separated ourselves from the communion of the Catholic Church—a grievous accusation, I confess, if it were true; for we acknowledge that there is no salvation to be expected ordinarily without the pale of the Church. But when all things are judicially weighed in the balance of right reason, when it shall appear that we never had any such foreign Patriarch for the first six hundred years and upwards, and it was a gross violation of the canons of the Catholic Church to attempt after that to obtrude any such jurisdiction upon us; that before the bishops of Rome ever exercised any jurisdiction in Britain, they had quitted their lawful patriarchate, wherewith they were invested by the authority of the Church, for an unlawful monarchy pretended to belong unto them by the institution of Christ; that whatsoever the Popes of Rome gained upon us in after ages, without our own free consent, was mere tyranny and usurpation; that our kings with their Synods and Parliaments had power to revoke, retract, and abrogate whatsoever they found by experience to become burdensome and insupportable to their subjects; that they did use in all ages, with the consent of the Church and Kingdom of England to limit and restrain the exercise of papal power, and to provide remedies against the daily encroachments of the Roman Court; so as Henry VIII. at the Reformation did but tread in the steps of his most renowned ancestors, who flourished while Popery was in its zenith, and pursued but that way which they had chalked out unto him—a way warranted by the practice of the most Christian emperors of old, and frequented at this day by the greatest, or rather by all the princes of the Roman communion so often as they find occasion—when it shall be made evident that the Bishops of Rome never enjoyed any quiet or settled possession of that power which was after deservedly cast out of England, so as to beget a lawful prescription—and lastly, that we have not at all separated ourselves from the communion of the Catholic Church, nor of any part thereof, Roman or other, *qua tales*, as they are such, but only in their innovations, wherein they have separated themselves first from their common mother and from the fellowship of their own sisters—I say, when all this shall be cleared, and the schism is brought home and laid at the right door, then we may safely conclude that by how much we should turn more Roman than we are (whilst things continue in the same condition), by so much we should render ourselves less Catholic, and plunge ourselves deeper into schism whilst we seek to avoid it.'

'Whosoever doth preserve his obedience entire to the universal Church and its representative, a General Council, and to all his superiors in their due order, so far as by law he is obliged; who holds an internal communion with all churches, and an external communion so far as he can with a good conscience; who approves no reformation but that which is made by lawful authority, upon sufficient grounds, with due moderation; who derives his Christianity by the uninterrupted line of apostolical succession; who contents himself with his proper place in the ecclesiastical body; who disbelieves nothing in Holy Scripture, and if he hold any errors unwittingly and unwillingly, doth implicitly renounce them by his fuller and more firm adherence to that infallible rule . . . This man may truly say, "My name is Christian, my surname is Catholic."' 'I make not the least doubt that the Church of England before the Reformation, and the Church of England after the Reformation, are as much the same Church as a garden before it is weeded and after it is weeded is the same garden; or a vine before it is pruned and after it is pruned and freed from the luxuriant branches is one and the same vine.'

This is the defence of the Reformation from what is called the Anglo-Catholic point of view. As to those who have defended it on the purely Protestant ground, viz. on the right of private judgment, and the obligation on every man to fashion his belief simply in accordance with the Scriptures, their name is Legion. The most famous doctor of this school is William Chillingworth, who in his great work, 'The Bible the Religion of Protestants,' has produced a treatise of marvellous power and acuteness.

The Protestant defence— William Chillingworth

The attempts to restrain religious thought to the basis of the Prayer-book and Articles of the Reformation settlement were long continued, but were never entirely successful. The variety and eccentricity of religious views, which have been its product, have often been made a subject of reproach against the Reformation. It may be questioned however whether this is justly a subject for reproach. The restraint of religious thought by penal laws, or church censures, or social disabilities, is more likely to impede the progress of religion, by producing discontent, indifference, and secret unbelief, than the perfect freedom given to every man to hold, advocate, and practise what he believes to be the truth in the way which he thinks best. A scope for earnestness and zeal is thus provided, and in the torrent which arises from the confluence of various streams of earnestness, the reformed Church of England is well able to hold her own and to maintain her progress.

Varieties of doctrine no just reproach to the Reformation

Writers unfriendly to the Church of England have endeavoured to cast a slur upon the Reformation by magnifying and dwelling upon the confusion, shortcomings, and irregularities which were prevalent in England, in religious matters, during the first years of Elizabeth's reign. Nothing could well be more unphilosophical or more unfair than such treatment. Is it conceivable that the Church, the nation, the government, the law, the political and social conditions of affairs, could pass through such a revolution, as that which met them at this time, without great confusion, irregularity, and disorder? Is it to be imagined that from the mass priests of Mary's reign, and the few hundred Protestant refugees, many of whom were violent fanatics, a decent, orthodox, and learned incumbent could at once be found

The reformed Church unfairly censured for irregularities

for each of the ten thousand parishes of England—that sermons advocating the doctrines of the Prayer-book should at once be heard in every pulpit—that a comely and rubrical service should at once be seen in every church? The notion is simply preposterous. And yet it is not thought beneath the dignity of history to taunt the Church of England because she did not show herself at once perfectly armed and equipped to take the place of the exploded superstitions of Rome. Rather it is a subject of wonder to the true historian, and of earnest thankfulness to the true member of the Church, that out of the apparent chaos and the manifest difficulties, so much order and light was so soon educed.

Among these difficulties not the least was the character of Elizabeth, and the policy towards which she was constantly veering during the earlier years of her reign. It is not too much to say that the Reformation forced Elizabeth into being a great Sovereign, as it certainly brought England into the position of a great nation. The character of Elizabeth is one of the most singular compounds to be found in all history. With great abilities, keen insight, a most determined will and perfect courage, she yet was extraordinarily vacillating of purpose, and liable to be swayed by the lowest impulses, while she was deficient both in moral strictness and in religious conviction. For a considerable time, at the beginning of her reign, she hovered on the verge of becoming even a more contemptible Sovereign than her sister, when, carried away by her mad love for Lord Robert Dudley, she was almost prepared to sacrifice the cause of the Reformation, if she might obtain the support of the

Difficulty arising from the character of Elizabeth

King of Spain for her union with Dudley. What was it that saved her from this step, which would have been absolutely fatal to the country? It was that keen political insight which never quite deserted her, and soon taught her that England, which had welcomed back the reformed faith in place of the late horrors, and which utterly detested Spain and Spanish principles, would have at once hurled her from her throne, had she ventured thus to degrade herself and her country. It was then that she learned the force of that spirit and those principles which were represented by her great ministers Cecil and Bacon, and knew that the religious sentiment of the best and wisest of the English people was not a thing to be trifled with, as the caprices of self-interest or the shufflings of State policy might suggest, but must be loyally supported and upheld, or the throne itself would totter. Not that Elizabeth, even in her most complacent moods, was altogether a nursing mother to the Church of England. She never entirely liked its settlement. She was too worldly to appreciate its doctrine, too sensuous to enjoy the plainness of its ritual. She could not get over her objections to the married clergy; and she had no patience with the bishops for not enforcing a discipline which her own courtiers made impossible. She had no scruple in robbing the Church of its property, and she cared little whether the people had a sufficiency of instruction or not. But substantial and efficient support she gave to it, and identified herself and her policy with the cause of which it was the brightest ornament. It was thus that she became a great Queen and England became a great nation. Her political insight was sufficiently strong to overcome any tendencies which she had to take a different course. Had she done so—had she left 'religion in England unchanged, merely attempting to modify the fanaticism of the Catholics by some practical toleration,' she would have 'drifted on in happy insignificance till some fresh ascendency of Ultramontanism and persecution had been followed by rebellion and civil war. . . . The temptation to this to a common nature would have been irresistible, and that Elizabeth remained in essentials true to the Reformation to which she owed her birth and Crown, must never be forgotten when we are provoked to condemn her inconsistencies.'[1]

The cruelty undoubtedly exercised towards the Romanists during the reign of Elizabeth has often been made a subject of reproach to the Reformation, and it has even been contended that the severities shown were as great as those experienced by the reformers during the reign of Mary.

The Reformation not chargeable with the cruelties exercised towards Romanists

In the first place, it should not be forgotten that taking the highest number of Romanists alleged to have been put to death under Elizabeth, the average scarcely exceeds four for each year of her reign; whereas, under Mary, during the four years of persecution, the average nearly reaches seventy. In the next place, it is certain that no Romanists suffered under Elizabeth simply for what was called heresy. The executions were for treasonable complicity with the enemies of England, or for disobedience to the secular laws. Without attempting to justify this policy, it may fairly be asserted that the Reformation, as such, is not responsible for it. Whether or not the unex-

[1] Froude, *History of England*, vii. 263.

ampled difficulties with which Elizabeth's ministers had to contend could have been overcome by some other means, it is clear that there is nothing in the reformed faith which encourages persecution. That individuals, especially some of the Puritanical party, called for severe measures against the Romanists, does not disprove this. Toleration is of the very essence of the Reformation, when rightly understood; just as it is essentially opposed to the principles of Romanism. It needed indeed a somewhat long education before this great truth could be reached—before the mistakes of Laud were corrected by the higher wisdom of Jeremy Taylor—but the credit of having taught it to the world is certainly due to the Reformation.

This great movement, not in itself or at its commencement favourable to literature, art, and science, being of necessity narrow, intense, and antagonistic, became nevertheless, on its success and settlement, the parent of all that is greatest and best in the triumphs of human intellect.

Its effects favourable to art and literature

Nor should its indirect effect upon the Church of Rome be overlooked. It destroyed in it the paganised religion of the sixteenth century, to bring out a more earnest, devout, and energetic habit; which, if still more opposed to the spirit of the Reformation than the older form, has been constrained to depend for its progress not on burnings and the Inquisition, but on a rivalry in good works and zeal for religion.

Its effect on the Roman Church

INDEX

INDEX.

ABBOTS

ABBOTS, the greater, not opposed to suppression of smaller monasteries, 32; hanging of twelve of, 34

Act, Consecration, the, 16; for restraint of appeals, the, 16; of supremacy of Henry VIII. 17; to regulate trials for heresy, 23; Treason, the, atrocious character of, 26; of Six Articles, the, making of, 51; character of, 53; ordering Communion in both kinds, 65; to give colleges and chantries to Crown, 67, 96; of Uniformity, the first, 72; the second, 93; against 'vagabonds,' 95; to legalise clerical marriage, 97; for securing tithes, 97; for removal of images and pictures, 98; for holidays, 99; of Supremacy, of Elizabeth, 161; of Uniformity, of Elizabeth, 159, 163; changes made in Prayer-book by, 159, 163

A Lasco, John, called to England by Cranmer, 69; friendship of Cranmer for, 83

Aless, Mr., at the meeting of bishops, 46; Latin Prayer-book of, 164

BARLOW

Altars, first removed by Ridley, 66; order of Council to remove, 78

Articles, the Ten, 41; the Thirteen, 50 *note*; the Forty-two, formation of, 82; accepted by Convocation, 83; review of, 193; the Eleven, 183, 193; the Thirty-nine, before Convocation, 194; ratification by the Queen of, 195; changes introduced into, 195; attempt to enforce subscription of, 195; stayed by the Queen, 196; Act to enforce, passed, 197; revision of in Convocation, 197; subscription of, 198

Augmentation, Court of, 33

Augsburg, Confession of, refused by King Henry, 44

Aylmer, Archdeacon, defends reformed doctrine, 116

Ayscough, Anne, martyrdom of 38

BACON, Lord Keeper, speech by, 160

Barlow, Bishop, gives manors to Somerset, 104; one of the consecrators of Parker, 171

BARNES

Barnes, Dr., lends church to Latimer, 20; in trouble for Lutheranism, 22; writes against Sir T. More, 22

Barton, Elizabeth, Nun of Kent, affair of, 25

Becke, Thomas, rifling of tomb of, 49

Benefices, spoliation of, 106; destitution of, 107

Bible, English, the first, 28; Matthew's 49; the Great, 49; order for English to be set up in churches, 49, 63

Bidding Prayer, the new form of, 64

Bilney, Thomas, martyrdom of, 20

Bishops, the, support the King in the divorce case, 19; endeavour to suppress Tyndale's version of the New Testament, 24; jurisdiction of suspended, 29, 66; not opposed to the suppression of monasteries, 32; the imprisoned, released by Queen Mary, 115; the reformed, dispossessed by Queen Mary, 115; committed to prison, 117; measures taken against, 118; reproved by Queen Mary's Council for slackness, 129; the Romish, treatment of, under Elizabeth, 166–168; consecration of reforming, under Elizabeth, 172; poverty of sees of, 172; scrupulousness of, 175; not favourable to discipline, 184

Boleyn, Anne, divorce of, decreed by the Convocations, 53

Bonner, Bishop, committed to prison, 64; deprivation of, 75; release of, 115; persecuting measures of, 129; treatment of Archdeacon Philpot by, 137

Boucher, Joan, execution of, 111

Bradford, John, imprisonment of, 127

CLERGY

Bramhall, Archbishop, defence of the Church of England by, 205

Bridewell, palace of, given by King Edward for public uses, 110

Bucer, Martin, made professor at Cambridge, 69

CALVIN, John, opinion of, on English Prayer-book, 147

Camden, William, estimate by, of the morality of King Edward's time, 112

Canterbury, cathedral of, spoliation of, 110; burnings of reformers at, 129, 141

Carranza, Bartolomeo de, comes with Philip to England, 110; Queen's confessor, 121; visitation of the universities by, 121; manages trial of Cranmer, 132

Carthusian monks, the, persecution of, 27

Castro, Alphonso de, comes with Philip to England, 120; preaches in favour of toleration, 122–128

Catechism, Lutheran, published by Cranmer, 80; Poynet's, 84

Cecil, Sir W., checks violent reformers, 157

Cheyney, Bishop, defends reformed doctrine, 116; refuses to subscribe Articles, 197

Chillingworth, William, 'The Religion of Protestants' of, 208

Churches, spoliation of, at Reformation, 108, 109

Clergy, the English, Acts to regulate, 10; Royal Supremacy voted by, 13, 17; submission of, 14; petition against annates by, 15; change in position of, 17; vote illegality of the King's marriage, 17; re-

COLET

pudiate the Pope, 18; opposed to use o English Prayer-book, 74; generally conform under Queen Elizabeth, 169; great want of, 170; ordinations of, 173; discouragement of marriage of, 177; oppose Parker's discipline, 188; the London 'Reply' of, 189; the unconformable, 189, 190

Colet, Dean, 6, 19

Commission of bishops to try heretics, 124

Commissioners for suppressing smaller monasteries, 33; for visiting the greater, 34; to construct First English Liturgy, 65; to seize colleges and chantries, 104; for taking Church goods, 108; to review the Prayer-books of Edward VI. 156; Protestant spirit of, 157; checked by Cecil, 157; to conduct visitation under Queen Elizabeth, 169, 180, 181; declaration tendered by, 181

Communion, Holy, to be administered in both kinds, 65; office of, 66; office of, in first Prayer-book, 71, 92; in second Prayer-book, 92, 93; in Elizabethan Prayer-book, 158

Confession to priest, treatment of, in Ten Articles, 41

Consecration Statute, the, 16

Convocation of Canterbury, the, reply of to the charges against ordinaries, 14; submission of to the King's Articles, 15; petition of against Papal annates, 15; accepts Royal Supremacy, 13; votes supply, 13; votes marriage of Henry and Catherine illegal, 17; repudiates the Pope, 17; accepts the Ten Articles, 43; protests against Council of Mantua, 44; votes diminution of saints'

CRANMER

days, 45; commences revision of Liturgy, 56; endeavours to check proceedings at beginning of Edward VI.'s reign, 61; decrees the administering of Communion in both kinds, 65; Committee of, draws up Communion Service, 65; accepts the Forty-two Articles, 83; sanctions first English Prayer-book, 71; sanctions second Prayer-book, 84; under Mary upholds Roman doctrine, 116; under Elizabeth opposed to changes, 155; debate in a, as to ceremonial, 185

Convocation of York accepts Royal Supremacy, 13; votes supply, 13; votes marriage of Henry and Catherine illegal, 17; repudiates the Pope, 17

Court of High Commission established by Parliament, 161

Coverdale, Bishop, makes first translation of Bible, 28; one of the consecrators of Parker, 171

Cox, Dr., one of Committee for first Prayer-book, 65; goes to Frankfort, 147; establishes use of English Prayer-book, 148

Cranmer, Archbishop, interview of with Fryth, 23; appointment of to Primacy, 24; pronounces divorce sentence, 24; arranges for revision of translation of Bible, 49; brings Lutheran divines to England, 50; procures divorce of Anne of Cleves, 53; retains favour with King Henry VIII. 54, 57; work of in Liturgical revision, 54; opinions of, 60; invites foreign divines to England, 69; publishes Catechism of Justice Jonas, 80; writes treatise on the Eucharist, 81; insists upon the execution of

CRUMWELL

Joan Boucher, 111; bitterness of Queen Mary against, 118; sent to Oxford to dispute, 118; degradation of, 132; recantations signed by, 133; retractation of recantations by, 134; last speech of, 134; burning of, 135; character of, 135

Crumwell, Thomas, rise of, 25; Reformation advanced by, 25; scheme of against More and Fisher, 25; endeavours of to influence public opinion, 27; procures publication of English Bible, 28; appointed Vicar-General, 29; suggests suppression of monasteries, 30; acts as Vicar-General, 43; procures the making of the 'Institution of a Christian Man,' 45; attainder of, 53

Day, Bishop, refuses to remove altars, 79; committed to prison, 79; release of, 115

Declaration, tendered by Commissioners, 181; drawn up by bishops, 183

Divines, foreign, amount of influence of on English Prayer-book, 70

Edward VI., King, commencement of reign of, 60; opinions of on Eucharist, 91; benefactions of, 110; death of, 112

Elizabeth, Queen, accession of, 151; policy of, 152; religious views of, 154, 175, 176; 'further order' taken by in the Church ceremonial, 165; speech of to Romish bishops, 167; opposed to marriage of clergy, 177; letter of to Archbishop Parker, 186; ratifies Thirty-

GRAMMAR

nine Articles, 195; character of, creates difficulties for the Church, 210, 211

Erasmus, Desiderius, satires of, 6; Greek Testament published by, 24; Paraphrases of to be set up in churches, 63

'Erudition of any Christian Man,' the, making of, 54; character of, 55; accepted by Convocation, 55

Eucharist, the treatment of in Ten Articles, 42; in the 'Institution' and 'Erudition,' 55

Farrar, Bishop, burning of, 128

Field, Dean, defence of the Church of England by, 204

Fisher, Bishop, opposes Church reform, 11; implicated in affair of Nun of Kent, 25; refuses the oath of succession, 26; committed to Tower, 26; offer of a cardinal's hat to, 27; trial and execution of, 27

Fryth, John, a member of Cardinal's College, 22; writes against Sir T. More, 22; martyrdom of, 23

Gardiner, Bishop, *De Verâ Obedientiâ* of, 28; opponent of Cranmer, 57; committed to Fleet prison, 64; opinion of on first Prayer-book, 91; deprivation of, 105; release of, 115; policy of, 117–119

Gascoigne, Thomas, Dictionary of, 7 and *note*

Geneva, English Reformers at, 145, 148, 150

Gilpin, Bernard, preaches before the Commissioners, 180

Grace, Pilgrimage of, 34, 45

Grammar schools erected after suppression of monasteries, 36; by Edward VI. 110

GUEST

Guest, Dr., a commissioner to review Prayer-book, 157; answers Sir W. Cecil's paper, 158

HADDON, Dean, defends reformed doctrine, 116; translates Prayer-book into Latin, 164
Heath, Archbishop, refuses to sign Ordinal, 76; committed to Fleet prison, 76; release of, 115; speaks against Act of Supremacy, 162
Henry VIII., King, summons bishops before him, 11; influences Parliament, 11; grants pardon to clergy, 13; requires clergy to accept Three Articles, 14; visitatorial power given to, 17; firstfruits and tenths given to, 17; favour of to Latimer, 21; exasperation of against More and Fisher, 27; appoints Crumwell Vicar-General, 29; cruelty of towards abbots, 35; cruelties of the latter part of the reign of, 38; makes draft of Ten Articles, 41, 43; signs the 'Institution of a Christian Man,' 46-48; injunctions of, 49; excommunication of, 50; procures passing of Six Article Law, 51; favour of towards Cranmer, 54, 57; Primer of, 56; mistaken view of as to Supremacy, 59
Homilies, the first, 62, 80; the second, 198
Hooker, Richard, defence of the Church of England by, 203
Hooper, Bishop, laments growth of wild opinions, 68; character and opinions of, 88; refuses episcopal vestments, 89; conduct of in prison, 90; consecration of, 90; holds See of

LATIMER

Gloucester *in commendam*, 105; trial of, 125; burning of, 125
Hospitals, London, endowment of, 111

IGNORANCE of people at time of the Reformation, 39, 40
Images, treatment of, in Ten Articles, 42; in 'Institution of a Christian Man,' 47; orders to take away, 49, 63; treatment of, in Elizabethan Injunctions, 178
Injunctions, Royal, of 1536, 45; of 1538, 49; first of Edward VI. 63; second of Edward VI. 75; of Mary, 116; of Elizabeth, 177
'Institution of a Christian Man,' making of, 46; contents of, 47; reception of, 48
Insurrections in 1549, 73
'Interpretations,' the, of Archbishop Parker, 182

JEWEL, Bishop, 'Apology for the Church of England' of, 201
Justification, treatment of in Ten Articles, 42; in 'Institution of a Christian Man,' 46, 47

KITCHEN, Bishop, despoils See of Llandaff, 105: refuses to consecrate Parker, 171
Kneeling at Holy Communion, movement against, 93
Knox, John, ministers at Frankfort, 146; expelled by the city, 148; adopts Geneva discipline, 148

LAMBERT or Nicholson, burning of, 51
Latimer, Bishop, at Cambridge 20; preaches before the King,

LEVER

21; Rector of West Kington, 21; before Convocation, 21; Bishop of Worcester, 22; sermon of before Convocation, 40; preaches against spoliation of benefices, 107; against immorality of the time, 112; sent to Oxford to dispute 118; trial of, for heresy, 129–131; burning of, 131

Lever, minister at Frankfort, 147

Lutheran divines, negotiations with, 50

MANORS, episcopal, seizure of, 104

Mantua, Council of, protested against, 44

Martyr, Peter, made professor at Oxford, 69

Mary, Queen, accession of, 113; character of, 114; marriage of, 120; letter of as to punishment of heretics, 123; benefactions of, 141; unhappy condition of, 141; death of, 141

Monasteries, suppression of suggested by Crumwell, 30; decay of, 31; suppression of resolved on, 31; slanderous accusations against, 32; Act for suppression of the smaller, 32; arrangements for demolition of the smaller, 33; number of, 33; amount of opposition to demolition of, 33; the greater endangered by Pilgimage of Grace, 34; surrender of many of the greater, 34; acts of injustice in suppression of, 35; revenue obtained from, 33–35; uses made of some, 33–35; effects of dissolution of, 36

PLURALITIES

Monks and nuns, hard case of, on dissolution, 37

More, Sir T., Chancellorship of, 21; writes against Barnes, 22; against Tyndale, 23; implicated in affair of Nun of Kent, 25; refuses the oath of succession, 26; committed to Tower, 26; trial and execution of, 27

ORDINAL, the first reformed, 76 the second, 76, 77

Ordinaries, the grievance against, 13

Osmund, St., 'Custom Book' of, 8

PAPAL JURISDICTION, vote of clergy against, 18

Parker, Archbishop, absent from the review of the Prayer book, 157; appointment of as Primate, 170; consecration of, 171; consecration of bishops by, 172; difficulties of, 185; Advertisements of, 187, 188

Parliament of 1529, legislation of, 10; of Edward VI., legislation of, 64, 95, 100; of Mary, resists changes in religion, 115; the first of Elizabeth, 163

Parre, George Van, execution of, 111

Paul III., Pope, excommunication by of King Henry VIII. 44, 50

Petition of members of Parliament to Pope, 12

Philip, King, character of, 120

Phillips, Dean, defends reformed doctrine, 116

Philpot, Archdeacon, defends reformed doctrine, 116; trials of, 136; burning of, 138

Pluralities, Act to regulate, 11

Pole, Cardinal, kept back from proceeding to England, 117; arrival of in England, 122; absolves the Parliament and Convocation, 123; condemnation of at Rome, 141; death of, 141

Præmunire statute, clergy convicted under, 13

Prayer-book, the first English, character of, 71; accepted by Convocation, 71; established by law, 72; preface of, 73; disliked by violent reformers, 73; attempts to give it the character of the old services, 74; not objected to by Cranmer and Ridley, 87; review of, 91

Prayer-book, the second English, making of, 91; order for use of, 94

Prayer-book, the Elizabethan, formation of, 156, 163; the Latin, 164; use of English book ordered, 169

Primer, the first reforming, 29; of King Henry VIII. 56; of King Edward VI. 85

Processions, disuse of, ordered, 64

Proclamation against Bulls from Rome, 12; of the King's style and title, 18; to abolish authority of Pope, 18; numerous of 1548, 67; by Queen Elizabeth against changes in religion, 152

Proctors and pardoners, Act against, 12

Purgatory, doctrine of, attacked by Simon Fish, 4; defended by Sir T. More, 4; treatment of in Ten Articles, 43; in 'Institution of a Christian Man,' 46

Puritan, beginning of the name of, 190

Readers, ordinations of, 173; appointment of lay, 174

Reformation, the English, character of, 1-7: religious causes of, 2; political causes, 4; social causes, 5; assertion of national rights by, 8; legislation of, 9; advocates of, 18; advanced by Queen Mary's persecution, 113, 140; completion of settlement of, 199; defence of, 201; varieties of doctrine no reproach to, 209; irregularities of unavoidable, 209; not chargeable with cruelties to Romanists, 212; effects of favourable to art and literature, 213; effects of, on Roman Church, 213

Reformers, at Cambridge, 19; writings of, 86; triumph of in second Prayer-book, 93; objection of to kneeling at Holy Communion, 93; constancy of under persecution, 136; number of burned under Queen Mary, 139; the English, abroad, 143, 149; proceedings of those settled at Frankfort, 144, 145, 147-9; invite others to join them, 145; refuse to use English Prayer-book, 146; disputes as to discipline among, 148; become Presbyterians, 149; return of at death of Queen Mary, 150; alarm of at first proceedings under Elizabeth, 158

Restraint of appeals, Act for, 16

Revision of Liturgy, commencement of, 56

Ridley, Bishop, removes altars in Rochester diocese, 66; views on the Eucharist of, 88; uses second Prayer-book at St. Paul's, 94; sent to Oxford to dispute, 118; trial of for heresy, 129; burning of, 132

ROGERS

Rogers, John, makes translation of the Bible, 49; burning of, 125

Romanists, treatment of under Elizabeth, 191, 192, 212

Rubrick, the Black, inserted by Council, 93

SACRAMENTS, three, in Ten Articles, 42; seven, in 'Institution of a Christian Man,' 47

Salcot, Bishop, grants long leases of his manors, 105

Salisbury, Countess of, execution of, 38

Sampson, Dr., argues for Royal Supremacy, 28; gives up episcopal manors, 105

Saunders, Laurence, burning of, 128

Savoy, Hospital of, revenues of, given for charitable purposes, 110

Sees, six, founded after suppression of monasteries, 35

Service-books, the old, Order to destroy, 77

Services, unauthorised, use of, 67

Somerset, Duke of, religious views of, 60; seizes ecclesiastical buildings, 103

Somerset House, building of, 103

Soto, Pedro de, comes with Philip to England, 120

Spoliation of Church property in mediæval times, 101; at Reformation, various kinds of, 102, 104, 105, 108

Stafford, Mr., at Cambridge, 19

Supremacy, Royal, voted by the clergy, 13, 17; Act of, 17; delegation of to Crumwell, 29; mistaken views of, 59;

ZURICH

exercise of by Mary, 116; explanation of in Elizabethan Injunctions; 179

TAYLOR, Dr. Rowland, burning of, 126

Testament, the New, translated by Tyndale, 23

Tithes, impropriate, given to laymen, 36

Tonstal, Bishop, judges Bilney, 20; argues against Lutheran divines, 51; spoliation of the See of, 106; imprisonment of, 106; release of, 115

Tyndale, William, writes against Sir T. More, 23; translation of the Scriptures by, 23; martyrdom of, 24

VILLAGARCIA, Juan de, comes with Philip to England, 120; sent to Oxford as Professor, 121

Visitation, the first, under Edward VI. 61; the second, of Edward VI. 75; under Elizabeth, 186

Visitatorial powers given to the Crown, 17

Voysey, Bishop, loses property of his See, 105; imprisonment of, 106; release of, 115

WESTMINSTER ABBEY threatened by Somerset, 103

Whiting, Abbot, tragical fate of, 35

Wolsey, Cardinal, fall of, 9; inauguration of Church Reform by, 10; favours Lutherans, 19

Wycliffe, John, translation of Scriptures by, 23

ZURICH, the Reformers at, 145, 146